GOODSON MUMBA

THE LEAN PLAY BOOK

Strategies for Operational Excellence

Copyright © 2024 by Goodson Mumba

All rights reserved. No part of this publication may be reproduced, stored or transmitted in any form or by any means, electronic, mechanical, photocopying, recording, scanning, or otherwise without written permission from the publisher. It is illegal to copy this book, post it to a website, or distribute it by any other means without permission.

First edition

ISBN: 9798334901506

This book was professionally typeset on Reedsy. Find out more at reedsy.com

Contents

	Preface	iv
	Acknowledgement	vii
	Dedication	viii
	Disclaimer	ix
1	Chapter 1: Introduction to Lean Management	1
2	Chapter 2: Identifying Value	20
3	Chapter 3: Value Stream Mapping	42
4	Chapter 4: Eliminating Waste	62
5	Chapter 5: Continuous Improvement (Kaizen)	81
6	Chapter 6: Just-In-Time (JIT) Production	98
7	Chapter 7: Lean Tools and Techniques	116
8	Chapter 8: Lean Leadership and Culture	133
9	Chapter 9: Lean Metrics and Performance Measurement	150
10	Chapter 10: Lean in Manufacturing	167
11	Chapter 11: Lean in Service Industries	184
12	Chapter 12: Lean in Healthcare	203
13	Chapter 13: Lean in Supply Chain Management	221
14	Chapter 14: Digital Transformation and Lean	239
15	Chapter 15: Sustaining Lean Improvements	261
	About the Author	287

Preface

Welcome to *The Lean Playbook: Strategies for Operational Excellence*. This book is a comprehensive guide crafted for leaders, practitioners, and enthusiasts embarking on a journey towards transformative change in their organizations through Lean management principles.

In today's dynamic and competitive business landscape, the pursuit of operational excellence is not merely a goal but a necessity for survival and growth. The Lean methodology, rooted in principles of continuous improvement, waste reduction, and respect for people, offers a proven path to achieving sustainable success. Whether you are in manufacturing, healthcare, services, or any industry, the principles and practices of Lean are universally applicable, providing a framework for optimizing processes, enhancing quality, and delivering greater value to customers.

This playbook is designed to be your companion, offering practical insights, real-world case studies, and actionable strategies to implement Lean effectively. From understanding the foundational principles of Lean to mastering advanced tools like Value Stream Mapping, Kaizen, and JIT production, each chapter equips you with the knowledge and tools needed to drive meaningful change.

Through the pages of this book, you will explore:

- **The Origins and Evolution of Lean:** Trace the historical roots of Lean and understand how it has evolved into a cornerstone of modern management philosophy.
- **Key Principles of Lean:** Delve into the core principles that underpin Lean thinking and learn how they can be applied to achieve operational excellence.
- **Practical Implementation Strategies:** Gain insights into practical methodologies and frameworks for implementing Lean across various organizational functions.
- **Case Studies and Success Stories:** Learn from real-world examples of organizations that have successfully implemented Lean, uncovering the challenges they faced and the strategies they employed to overcome them.
- **Tools and Techniques:** Explore a comprehensive toolkit of Lean tools and techniques, from 5S and Value Stream Mapping to Total Productive Maintenance (TPM) and beyond.

Moreover, this book goes beyond theory by addressing the critical aspects of Lean leadership, cultural transformation, and sustaining Lean improvements over the long term. It emphasizes the importance of engaging employees, fostering a culture of continuous improvement, and aligning Lean initiatives with strategic business goals.

Whether you are a seasoned Lean practitioner looking to refine your skills or a newcomer seeking to initiate a Lean transformation, *The Lean Playbook* offers something valuable for everyone. Our aim is to empower you with the knowledge, insights, and practical guidance needed to navigate the complexities of Lean implementation and achieve lasting success in your pursuit of operational excellence.

As you embark on this journey through the Lean playbook, I encourage you to embrace curiosity, collaboration, and a relentless commitment to improvement. Together, let us unlock the full potential of Lean and create a future where organizations thrive through continuous innovation and excellence.

Welcome to *The Lean Playbook: Strategies for Operational Excellence*—your roadmap to achieving operational excellence through Lean management.

Let's begin.

Goodson Mumba

Acknowledgement

I would like to eternally and gratefully acknowledge the Almighty God for the infinite intelligence from His universal mind where we draw from all that we come to know and are yet to know. May I also acknowledge and thank everyone that has played a part in my journey of life in terms of spiritual, moral, emotional and material support.

Dedication

I extend my sincerest gratitude to my beloved wife, Edith Mumba, and our children, Angelina, Lubuto, Letticia, Lulumbi, and Butusho, for their unwavering support and understanding throughout the conception, writing, and eventual publication of this book, despite the sacrifices and challenges they endured.

Disclaimer

This book is a work of fiction. Names, characters, businesses, places, events, and incidents are either the products of the author's imagination or used in a fictitious manner. Any resemblance to actual persons, living or dead, or actual events is purely coincidental.

1

Chapter 1: Introduction to Lean Management

Origins and History of Lean

Sarah Mitchell sat at the head of the long, polished conference table, scanning the faces of the executives gathered around her. As the newly appointed Chief Operating Officer of Aurora Electronics, she faced a formidable challenge: turning around a company plagued by inefficiencies and declining profits. The weight of the task ahead felt heavy, but Sarah was determined.

"Thank you all for being here," Sarah began, her voice steady. "Today, we embark on a journey to transform Aurora Electronics through Lean Management. But before we dive into the how, let's start with the why."

A few skeptical glances were exchanged among the executives. Raj Patel, the production manager, crossed his arms and leaned back in his chair, a frown etched on his face.

Sarah clicked a remote, and a projector displayed an image

of a bustling assembly line. "Our story begins in Japan, post-World War II. Toyota, then a struggling automobile manufacturer, needed to rebuild with limited resources. They developed a system that focused on eliminating waste, improving quality, and respecting people. This system came to be known as the Toyota Production System, or TPS, the foundation of Lean Management."

James Thompson, the Lean consultant Sarah had brought in, stepped forward. "Toyota's approach was revolutionary," he explained. "They identified seven types of waste – overproduction, waiting, transport, extra processing, inventory, motion, and defects. By relentlessly focusing on eliminating these wastes, they achieved incredible efficiency and quality."

The executives listened, some more intently than others. Sarah continued, "Lean is not just about cutting costs. It's about creating value for our customers by improving our processes. It's a mindset of continuous improvement, or 'Kaizen,' where every employee, from the CEO to the frontline worker, is engaged in making things better."

Lisa Chen, the HR director, nodded enthusiastically. "It sounds promising, but how do we start?"

James smiled. "We start with education and engagement. Understanding Lean's origins helps us appreciate its power. For instance, during the 1980s, Western companies like Ford and General Motors visited Japan to learn from Toyota. They saw firsthand how Lean could transform industries."

Sarah added, "Lean principles have since been applied beyond manufacturing. Healthcare, services, even government sectors have benefited from Lean thinking. It's about maximizing value and minimizing waste in any process."

Raj uncrossed his arms and leaned forward slightly. "But

how do we ensure it works for us? We've tried other improvement programs before."

"That's a valid concern," Sarah acknowledged. "Success requires commitment from all levels of the organization. It's about building a culture where everyone is empowered to identify and solve problems. We will start with small, manageable projects and scale up as we see success."

James projected a series of case studies showing companies that had transformed through Lean. "These examples show that when done right, Lean not only improves efficiency but also boosts employee morale and customer satisfaction."

Maria Gonzalez, a frontline worker and natural leader, was invited to share her thoughts. "I believe in continuous improvement. If Lean can help us reduce the daily frustrations and inefficiencies we face on the shop floor, I'm all in."

Sarah smiled, encouraged by Maria's support. "Thank you, Maria. Your enthusiasm is exactly what we need. Together, we can make Aurora a model of operational excellence."

As the meeting concluded, Sarah felt a renewed sense of optimism. The road ahead would be challenging, but with the principles of Lean as their guide, she believed Aurora Electronics could not only survive but thrive. This was just the beginning of their Lean journey.

Core Principles of Lean

The atmosphere in the training room was a mix of curiosity and skepticism. Aurora Electronics' leadership team, along with a few key managers and frontline workers, were gathered for the first official Lean Management workshop. Sarah Mitchell stood at the front of the room, a whiteboard behind her filled with diagrams and notes.

"Welcome, everyone," Sarah began. "Today, we'll delve into the core principles of Lean. Understanding these principles is crucial for our transformation."

James Thompson, the Lean consultant, stepped forward, holding a marker. "Lean is built on five core principles. These guide our actions and decisions. Let's explore each one."

He wrote on the whiteboard:

1. **Value**
2. **Value Stream**
3. **Flow**
4. **Pull**
5. **Perfection**

James turned to the group. "The first principle is **Value**. Value is defined by the customer. It's what they're willing to pay for. Everything we do must add value from the customer's perspective."

Lisa Chen raised her hand. "How do we determine what our customers value most?"

"Great question," James replied. "We engage with them. Surveys, feedback, direct conversations. We must understand their needs and expectations. Once we define value, we can focus on eliminating anything that doesn't contribute to it."

Sarah added, "For Aurora, this means reevaluating our products and services. Are we meeting our customers' needs effectively?"

James nodded and wrote the second principle. "Next is the **Value Stream**. This involves mapping out all the steps in our processes. From raw materials to finished product, we

CHAPTER 1: INTRODUCTION TO LEAN MANAGEMENT

identify every action. Then, we analyze which steps add value and which don't."

Raj Patel, the production manager, leaned forward. "So, we're looking for inefficiencies?"

"Exactly," James said. "We're identifying and eliminating waste. This creates a streamlined process where every step adds value."

James wrote the third principle. "The third principle is **Flow**. Once we've removed waste, we aim for a continuous flow of production. No bottlenecks, no interruptions. It's about creating a smooth process from start to finish."

Maria Gonzalez, the frontline worker, raised her hand. "What about unexpected issues? Machine breakdowns, supply delays?"

"Those are real challenges," James acknowledged. "Part of Lean is developing flexibility and problem-solving skills. We'll train everyone to quickly address and resolve these issues, maintaining flow."

James moved to the fourth principle. "The fourth principle is **Pull**. Instead of pushing products based on forecasts, we produce based on actual demand. This minimizes excess inventory and aligns production with customer needs."

Lisa looked intrigued. "So, we're producing exactly what's needed, when it's needed?"

"Correct," James said. "This approach reduces waste and ensures we're responsive to customer demand."

Finally, James wrote the fifth principle. "The last principle is **Perfection**. Lean is about continuous improvement. We're never fully 'done' improving. We constantly seek ways to enhance quality, efficiency, and value."

Sarah stepped forward. "Perfection is a journey, not a

destination. We'll cultivate a culture where everyone is empowered to suggest improvements and innovations. This mindset is key to our long-term success."

James handed out copies of a Value Stream Map. "Let's start with an exercise. We'll map out one of our key processes and identify areas of waste. This hands-on approach will help us understand how to apply these principles."

As the group worked on the exercise, discussions grew animated. Raj, initially skeptical, found himself identifying several inefficiencies in the current production line. Maria suggested practical solutions from her daily experiences on the shop floor.

After the exercise, James reconvened the group. "Excellent work. This is just the beginning. Applying these core principles will transform how we operate and create value."

Sarah closed the session. "Thank you all for your participation. Remember, Lean is about collaboration and continuous improvement. Let's take these principles to heart and start making impactful changes."

As the team left the training room, the atmosphere was noticeably different. There was a sense of purpose and excitement. The core principles of Lean had not only been understood but embraced. Aurora Electronics was on its way to operational excellence, guided by the foundational tenets of Lean Management.

The Importance of Lean in Today's Business Environment

Sarah Mitchell stood at the head of the conference table, facing her team. The room was filled with department heads and key managers, all ready to dive into the next phase of their Lean journey. The whiteboard behind her displayed the words "Importance of Lean in Today's Business Environment."

"Good afternoon, everyone," Sarah began, her voice carrying a mix of urgency and optimism. "We've covered the origins and core principles of Lean. Today, we'll explore why Lean is not just beneficial but essential in today's business landscape."

James Thompson, the Lean consultant, took over. "In a rapidly changing global market, companies face intense competition, fluctuating demands, and economic uncertainties. Lean provides a robust framework to navigate these challenges. Let's discuss how."

He clicked the projector, and a slide titled "Key Drivers for Lean Adoption" appeared:

1. **Global Competition**
2. **Customer Expectations**
3. **Economic Pressures**
4. **Technological Advancements**
5. **Sustainability**

James pointed to the first item. "Global competition means that businesses can no longer afford inefficiencies. Companies in countries with lower labor costs can often undercut prices. Lean helps us streamline operations, reduce costs, and improve quality, making us more competitive."

Raj Patel, the production manager, spoke up. "But we've always managed to stay afloat. Why is Lean so critical now?"

Sarah answered, "Staying afloat isn't enough, Raj. To thrive, we need to be agile and efficient. Lean enables us to respond quickly to market changes and customer needs."

James moved to the next point. "Customer expectations have evolved. Today's customers demand higher quality, faster delivery, and personalized products. Lean helps us meet these demands by focusing on value creation and waste elimination."

Maria Gonzalez, the frontline worker, nodded. "I've noticed customers asking for quicker turnaround times. Lean could help us meet these expectations without compromising quality."

James smiled. "Exactly, Maria. Lean processes ensure we can deliver high-quality products promptly."

He pointed to the third item. "Economic pressures, such as rising material costs and labor expenses, squeeze our margins. Lean helps us do more with less, maximizing resources and minimizing waste. This is crucial for maintaining profitability."

Lisa Chen, the HR director, added, "Economic stability isn't guaranteed. Lean practices can help us remain resilient during downturns and flexible during upswings."

James continued, "Technological advancements are reshaping industries. Lean integrates well with new technologies, enhancing productivity and efficiency. By embracing Lean, we're better positioned to leverage innovations like automation and data analytics."

Sarah interjected, "Our industry is evolving. If we don't adapt, we risk falling behind. Lean provides a framework to integrate new technologies seamlessly into our operations."

James pointed to the final item. "Sustainability is increasingly important. Lean practices promote environmental responsibility by reducing waste and optimizing resource use. This not only benefits the planet but also appeals to eco-conscious consumers and stakeholders."

Raj looked thoughtful. "So, Lean isn't just about internal efficiency. It's about staying relevant in a broader context."

James nodded. "Precisely. Lean helps us adapt to external pressures and stay ahead of the curve."

Sarah addressed the group. "Implementing Lean is a strategic imperative. It's about ensuring Aurora Electronics thrives in today's competitive, customer-driven, and technologically advanced environment. Let's discuss some examples."

James presented case studies of companies that had successfully adopted Lean, showing significant improvements in efficiency, customer satisfaction, and profitability. The room buzzed with interest as they saw real-world applications of Lean principles.

Sarah concluded the session. "Lean is our path forward. It's about making smart, sustainable changes that position us for long-term success. We've made a strong start by understanding its principles and importance. Now, let's commit to embedding Lean into our culture and operations."

As the meeting adjourned, the team felt a renewed sense of purpose. The importance of Lean in today's business environment was clear, and Aurora Electronics was ready to harness its power to become a leader in operational excellence.

Lean vs. Traditional Management

The training room was filled with the hum of conversation as employees gathered for the next workshop. The topic today was crucial: understanding the differences between Lean and traditional management. Sarah Mitchell and James Thompson stood at the front, ready to guide the team through this important comparison.

"Good morning, everyone," Sarah began, quieting the room. "Today, we'll compare Lean Management with Traditional Management. Understanding these differences will help us appreciate why we're moving towards Lean."

James took the floor, writing "Traditional Management" on one side of the whiteboard and "Lean Management" on the other. "Let's start with Traditional Management," he said. "This approach has been the standard for many years. Here are some key characteristics."

He listed the points under "Traditional Management":

1. **Hierarchical Structure**
2. **Top-Down Decision Making**
3. **Focus on Short-Term Goals**
4. **Large Batch Production**
5. **Cost Reduction Through Scale**
6. **Fixed Roles and Responsibilities**

James turned to the group. "Traditional Management relies on a hierarchical structure. Decisions are made at the top and passed down. This can lead to slow responses and a disconnect between management and frontline workers."

Raj Patel, the production manager, nodded. "That's how

we've always done things. It's worked, but it does feel rigid at times."

"Exactly," James replied. "Traditional management also focuses heavily on short-term financial goals. This often results in large batch production to maximize efficiency, but it can lead to excess inventory and waste."

Lisa Chen, the HR director, added, "Employees have fixed roles and responsibilities. There's little room for cross-functional collaboration or innovation."

James then shifted to the other side of the board. "Now, let's look at Lean Management."

He wrote the points under "Lean Management":

1. **Flat Structure**
2. **Bottom-Up Decision Making**
3. **Focus on Long-Term Goals**
4. **Small Batch Production**
5. **Value Creation Through Efficiency**
6. **Flexible Roles and Continuous Improvement**

James explained, "Lean Management favors a flat structure, promoting a culture where ideas and feedback flow freely from all levels. This bottom-up approach empowers employees to contribute to decision-making, fostering a sense of ownership and engagement."

Maria Gonzalez, the frontline worker, raised her hand. "So, our input will be valued more in a Lean system?"

"Absolutely, Maria," James affirmed. "In Lean, everyone's perspective is important. This inclusivity leads to better decision-making and quicker problem-solving."

Sarah stepped in. "Lean also emphasizes long-term goals

over short-term gains. We focus on sustainable growth and continuous improvement, ensuring we remain competitive and resilient."

James continued, "Small batch production is another key difference. By producing in smaller quantities, we reduce waste, improve quality, and respond more quickly to customer demands."

Raj looked intrigued. "That sounds efficient, but doesn't it increase costs?"

"Initially, it might seem so," James replied. "But over time, the reduction in waste and improvements in efficiency balance out the costs, leading to greater overall savings and customer satisfaction."

Sarah added, "Lean management also encourages flexible roles and continuous improvement. Employees are trained to handle various tasks, fostering a culture of innovation and adaptability."

James presented a slide with a side-by-side comparison of a traditional factory floor and a Lean one. "In traditional management, changes are often met with resistance. Lean creates an environment where change is part of the process, leading to a dynamic and responsive organization."

Lisa spoke up, "This shift sounds promising, but how do we transition from our current traditional system to a Lean one?"

Sarah smiled. "That's the journey we're on. We'll start with pilot projects, training, and gradually implement Lean principles across the organization. It's about taking measured steps and learning as we go."

James concluded, "Understanding these differences helps us see why Lean is more suited to today's fast-paced, customer-driven market. It's not just a set of tools; it's a mindset shift towards efficiency, collaboration, and continuous improvement."

As the session ended, there was a palpable sense of excitement and readiness in the room. The contrast between Lean and traditional management was clear, and the team at Aurora Electronics was eager to embrace this new way of working.

Key Benefits of Lean Management

The hum of machinery filled the air as Sarah Mitchell and James Thompson led a group of executives and managers on a tour of the production floor. This was no ordinary tour; it was a practical demonstration of how Lean principles could transform their operations. The team stopped at various stations, where James explained the potential benefits of Lean Management.

"Lean is not just about theory," James began. "It's about tangible, real-world benefits. Let's explore these key benefits through some practical examples."

They arrived at the assembly line, where Maria Gonzalez was overseeing a new 5S initiative. The area was organized, tools were neatly labeled, and workstations were spotless.

1. Increased Efficiency

James gestured to the orderly workspace. "One of the most immediate benefits of Lean is increased efficiency. By eliminating waste and optimizing processes, we streamline operations. Maria, how has the 5S initiative impacted your workflow?"

Maria smiled. "It's been incredible. Everything is where it should be, which saves us time. We're no longer searching for tools or dealing with clutter. Our productivity has noticeably improved."

Raj Patel, the production manager, nodded in agreement. "I've seen the difference. There's less downtime, and we're able to maintain a steady pace."

2. Improved Quality

They moved to the quality control station, where Lisa Chen, the HR director, was speaking with a team member. James pointed to a chart showing a decline in defects.

"Improved quality is another key benefit," he said. "Lean focuses on getting things right the first time. This reduces defects and rework, leading to higher-quality products. Lisa, can you share how this has affected our customer feedback?"

Lisa turned to the group. "Since implementing Lean practices, we've seen a significant drop in customer complaints. Our products are meeting higher standards, which is boosting customer satisfaction and loyalty."

3. Enhanced Employee Engagement

James led the group to a Kaizen board, where employees were posting suggestions for improvements. "Lean fosters a culture of continuous improvement and engages employees at all levels," he explained. "When workers feel valued and empowered, their engagement and morale improve."

Maria added, "It's true. We're encouraged to share our ideas, and management listens. It makes us feel like we're part of the solution, not just following orders."

4. Faster Response Times

The group moved to the inventory area, where shelves were neatly stocked with minimal excess. "Lean's Just-in-Time production reduces inventory levels and shortens lead times," James continued. "This means we can respond faster to customer demands and market changes."

Raj looked at the streamlined inventory. "We've already seen benefits here. We're not overproducing, and we can adjust quickly if there's a change in demand."

5. Cost Savings

Finally, James led the group to a chart displaying cost savings from various Lean initiatives. "All these benefits lead to significant cost savings. By reducing waste, improving quality, and increasing efficiency, we cut costs across the board."

Sarah concluded, "These savings can be reinvested into the company, whether it's for new technology, employee training, or expanding our product line. Lean management helps us do more with less, driving sustainable growth."

6. Competitive Advantage

James wrapped up the tour. "All these benefits contribute to a stronger competitive advantage. By being more efficient, responsive, and quality-focused, we position ourselves ahead of our competitors."

Lisa added, "Customers notice these improvements too. Our reputation for quality and reliability will grow, attracting more business."

As the tour ended, the team gathered for a final discussion. The tangible benefits of Lean Management were clear, and there was a growing excitement about the potential for Aurora Electronics.

Sarah addressed the group. "We've seen firsthand how Lean can transform our operations. It's not just about theory; it's about real improvements that benefit everyone – our employees, our customers, and our bottom line. Let's commit to this journey and make Aurora Electronics a model of operational excellence."

The team left the production floor energized and inspired,

ready to embrace Lean principles and drive the company towards a brighter, more efficient future.

Case Studies: Successful Lean Implementations

The boardroom was packed with Aurora Electronics' key leaders and managers, all eager to learn from real-world examples of Lean implementations. Sarah Mitchell stood at the front with James Thompson, ready to present compelling case studies. A projector displayed slides with the title "Case Studies: Successful Lean Implementations."

"Good morning, everyone," Sarah began, her voice reflecting the excitement in the room. "Today, we'll look at companies that have successfully adopted Lean Management. These case studies will show us what's possible and inspire our journey."

James took over, clicking to the first slide. "Our first case study is Toyota, the pioneer of Lean Management. Toyota's success with Lean, or the Toyota Production System, is legendary."

Case Study 1: Toyota

James narrated, "Post-World War II, Toyota faced severe resource constraints. They developed Lean principles to maximize efficiency and minimize waste. By focusing on continuous improvement and respect for people, Toyota revolutionized manufacturing."

Sarah added, "The results were remarkable. Toyota became known for high-quality, reliable vehicles. They consistently outperformed competitors in efficiency and innovation, setting industry standards."

The room buzzed with interest as James clicked to the next slide.

Case Study 2: Danaher Corporation

"Danaher Corporation is another great example," James continued. "They adopted Lean in the 1980s, using it to transform from a struggling business into a global leader in industrial and healthcare technologies."

He explained, "Danaher implemented the Danaher Business System, inspired by Lean principles. They focused on continuous improvement, waste elimination, and customer satisfaction. This approach led to significant growth, improved margins, and a culture of innovation."

Lisa Chen, the HR director, was intrigued. "How did they manage such a widespread transformation?"

James replied, "It was through strong leadership commitment and relentless focus on Lean principles. They empowered employees at all levels to contribute to continuous improvement."

Case Study 3: Virginia Mason Medical Center

The next slide featured Virginia Mason Medical Center. "Lean isn't just for manufacturing," James pointed out. "Virginia Mason Medical Center in Seattle applied Lean to healthcare, transforming patient care."

He continued, "Facing rising costs and patient safety concerns, Virginia Mason adopted Lean principles to streamline operations and improve care. They reduced patient wait times, increased safety, and significantly improved patient outcomes."

Raj Patel, the production manager, looked impressed. "So, Lean can be adapted to different industries effectively?"

"Absolutely," Sarah confirmed. "Lean is about process improvement, which is universal. Virginia Mason's success shows how adaptable and powerful Lean can be."

Case Study 4: Nike

James then presented the story of Nike. "In the 1990s, Nike faced challenges with overproduction and long lead times. They turned to Lean to address these issues."

He explained, "Nike implemented Lean manufacturing across their supply chain, focusing on waste reduction and increasing efficiency. This shift allowed them to respond faster to market trends, reduce inventory costs, and improve product quality."

Maria Gonzalez, the frontline worker, asked, "How did Lean affect their product innovation?"

James smiled. "Lean actually enhanced it. By streamlining processes, Nike could allocate more resources to design and development, leading to innovative products and faster market entry."

Case Study 5: Boeing

The final case study featured Boeing. "Boeing faced intense competition and production inefficiencies," James said. "They adopted Lean to overhaul their manufacturing processes."

He continued, "By implementing Lean, Boeing reduced assembly time, improved product quality, and lowered costs. The 737 production line, for instance, saw significant improvements, leading to increased market share and customer satisfaction."

Sarah concluded, "These case studies highlight the transformative power of Lean. From automotive to healthcare, and from consumer goods to aerospace, Lean principles drive efficiency, innovation, and customer satisfaction."

She looked around the room, her eyes meeting those of her colleagues. "We can achieve similar success here at Aurora Electronics. By committing to Lean, we can streamline our operations, improve quality, and enhance our competitiveness."

James added, "Remember, Lean is a journey. These companies succeeded through dedication and continuous improvement. We have the potential to do the same."

The room erupted in applause, filled with renewed energy and determination. The case studies provided a vision of what was possible, inspiring the team to fully embrace Lean Management.

As the meeting ended, Sarah felt a sense of optimism. Aurora Electronics was ready to embark on their Lean journey, guided by the successes of those who had gone before them.

Chapter 2: Identifying Value

Defining Customer Value

The sun filtered through the large windows of the Aurora Electronics conference room, where a diverse group of employees gathered for a crucial workshop on identifying customer value. The room was arranged with round tables to facilitate discussion, and the walls were lined with charts and sticky notes.

Sarah Mitchell and James Thompson stood at the front, ready to lead the session. Sarah opened the workshop, her enthusiasm contagious.

"Good morning, everyone," she began. "Today's session is all about understanding what our customers value. This is the first and most critical step in Lean Management. We must define value from the customer's perspective."

James nodded. "To create value, we need to know our customers' needs, desires, and expectations. Let's start by discussing who our customers are and what they value most."

He clicked a slide titled "Defining Customer Value." The slide showed images of various customer profiles: end consumers, retailers, and B2B clients.

Exercise 1: Customer Personas

"Let's break into groups," Sarah instructed. "Each group will focus on one customer segment. Discuss their needs, challenges, and what they value in our products."

The employees split into groups. Raj Patel, the production manager, joined the group focusing on end consumers. Maria Gonzalez, the frontline worker, sat with the team discussing B2B clients, while Lisa Chen, the HR director, joined the group working on retailers.

The room buzzed with activity. Raj's group started brainstorming.

"Our end consumers value reliability and innovation," Raj said. "They want products that work seamlessly and incorporate the latest technology."

One team member added, "They also care about design and usability. The product should be user-friendly and aesthetically pleasing."

Across the room, Maria's group was deep in discussion.

"Our B2B clients need consistency and timely delivery," Maria said. "They rely on our products for their operations, so any delay or defect can cause significant issues for them."

A colleague chimed in, "They also value strong customer support. They need to know they can count on us if they encounter problems."

Meanwhile, Lisa's group discussed retailers.

"Retailers want products that sell quickly," Lisa said. "They value good margins and low return rates. They also appreciate marketing support to help promote the products."

Another member added, "They need efficient supply chain management. Keeping their shelves stocked without overstocking is crucial."

After the discussions, Sarah and James reconvened the group. James wrote the key points on a whiteboard, creating a comprehensive list of customer values.

Exercise 2: Prioritizing Customer Values

"Great insights," James said. "Now, let's prioritize these values. Which ones are most critical for our customers? Each group, rank the values you've identified."

The groups worked on their rankings, debating the importance of each value. Raj's group decided that reliability and innovation were top priorities for end consumers. Maria's group prioritized consistency and customer support for B2B clients, while Lisa's group placed high importance on product sell-through and supply chain efficiency for retailers.

After the ranking exercise, Sarah addressed the entire room.

Discussion: Aligning Operations with Customer Value

"Defining and prioritizing customer values is essential," she said. "But the next step is aligning our operations to deliver these values. How do we ensure our processes meet these customer expectations?"

James nodded in agreement. "For instance, if reliability is crucial, we need robust quality control. If timely delivery is a priority, our supply chain must be optimized."

Raj spoke up, "This means re-evaluating our production processes. We need to eliminate any steps that don't add value from the customer's perspective."

Maria added, "And enhance our customer support systems. Ensuring we have knowledgeable and responsive teams in place is critical."

Lisa chimed in, "We should also consider our partnerships with retailers. Providing them with marketing support and efficient supply chain solutions will build stronger relationships."

Sarah concluded the session. "Understanding and defining customer value is the foundation of Lean Management. This workshop has provided us with valuable insights into what our customers truly need. Now, let's commit to aligning our operations to deliver that value."

James added, "Our next steps involve creating action plans based on these insights. We'll work together to implement changes that ensure we're always focused on delivering maximum value to our customers."

The team left the workshop energized and focused, ready to take the next steps in their Lean journey by putting the customer at the center of everything they do. Aurora Electronics was on its way to creating a customer-centric culture, driving operational excellence through the lens of Lean Management.

Value Stream Mapping

The workshop room was abuzz with excitement as Aurora Electronics' team gathered for a practical session on Value Stream Mapping. Long tables were set up with large sheets of paper, markers, sticky notes, and other materials necessary for the exercise. Sarah Mitchell and James Thompson were at the front, ready to guide the team through this crucial Lean tool.

Sarah began, "Welcome back, everyone. Now that we've defined customer value, it's time to map out how we deliver that value. Today, we're going to create Value Stream Maps for our key processes."

James took over, clicking to a slide titled "Value Stream Mapping." "Value Stream Mapping helps us visualize the flow of materials and information required to bring a product to the customer. It highlights areas of waste and opportunities for improvement."

Exercise 1: Mapping the Current State

"Let's start with the current state," Sarah instructed. "We'll map out our existing processes from start to finish. Each group will focus on a different product line."

The team split into smaller groups, each assigned to a specific product line. Raj Patel's group was tasked with mapping the assembly process of their flagship electronics product. Maria Gonzalez's group focused on the supply chain process for components, while Lisa Chen's team tackled the customer service workflow.

Raj's group gathered around a large sheet of paper. "Let's list all the steps involved in the assembly process," Raj began. "From receiving components to final quality checks."

The group started noting down each step on sticky notes and placing them on the paper. They mapped out the flow of materials, identifying bottlenecks and delays.

Meanwhile, Maria's group was deep in mapping the supply chain process. "We start with supplier orders," Maria said. "Then, we have shipping, receiving, and inventory management."

Lisa's group worked on the customer service workflow. "We handle customer inquiries, process returns, and manage warranties," Lisa outlined. They detailed each step, from initial contact to issue resolution.

As the groups worked, Sarah and James moved around the room, offering guidance and answering questions.

Exercise 2: Identifying Waste and Inefficiencies

Once the current state maps were complete, James called for attention. "Great job, everyone. Now, let's identify areas of waste and inefficiency. Look for steps that don't add value from the customer's perspective, such as delays, excess inventory, and unnecessary movements."

Raj's group noticed several areas of waste in their assembly process. "We have too much inventory waiting at each stage," Raj pointed out. "And there are delays in quality checks."

Maria's group identified issues in the supply chain. "There are frequent delays in receiving shipments from suppliers," Maria said. "And our inventory management system is outdated, causing further delays."

Lisa's group found inefficiencies in the customer service process. "There's a lot of back-and-forth between departments," Lisa noted. "And some steps could be automated to save time."

Exercise 3: Mapping the Future State

Sarah reconvened the group. "Now that we've identified waste, let's map out the future state. How can we streamline these processes to deliver more value to our customers?"

Raj's group brainstormed solutions for their assembly process. "We could implement Just-in-Time inventory to reduce waiting times," Raj suggested. "And streamline quality checks by integrating them into the assembly line."

Maria's group discussed improving the supply chain. "We need to enhance our supplier relationships," Maria said. "And upgrade our inventory management system to track shipments in real-time."

Lisa's group focused on customer service improvements. "Let's automate routine tasks," Lisa proposed. "And create a more cohesive workflow between departments to speed up resolutions."

The groups worked diligently, mapping out their improved processes. The future state maps showed streamlined workflows, reduced waste, and enhanced efficiency.

Presentation and Discussion

James called for attention once more. "Let's present our future state maps and discuss the improvements."

Raj's group went first, showcasing their streamlined assembly process. "By implementing Just-in-Time inventory and integrating quality checks, we can reduce delays and improve product flow," Raj explained.

Maria's group presented their enhanced supply chain. "With real-time tracking and better supplier relationships, we can minimize delays and manage inventory more efficiently," Maria said.

Lisa's group shared their improved customer service workflow. "Automation and a cohesive workflow will reduce response times and improve customer satisfaction," Lisa outlined.

Sarah wrapped up the session. "Excellent work, everyone. These future state maps show how we can deliver more value to our customers. Our next step is to develop action plans to implement these improvements."

James added, "Value Stream Mapping is a powerful tool for identifying inefficiencies and creating more value. By continually refining our processes, we'll stay ahead of the competition and better meet our customers' needs."

The team left the workshop energized and ready to implement their plans. Aurora Electronics was on a clear path towards operational excellence, driven by a deep understanding of customer value and a commitment to continuous improvement.

Differentiating Value-Added and Non-Value-Added Activities

The meeting room was lively with Aurora Electronics team members gathered around tables filled with charts and diagrams. The walls were covered with sticky notes from their previous Value Stream Mapping session. Sarah Mitchell and James Thompson stood at the front, ready to delve into the next crucial step: differentiating value-added from non-value-added activities.

Sarah began, "Welcome back, everyone. Now that we've mapped our processes, it's time to differentiate between value-added and non-value-added activities. This will help us focus on what truly matters to our customers."

James clicked to a slide titled "Value-Added vs. Non-Value-Added Activities." He explained, "Value-added activities are those that directly contribute to meeting customer needs. Non-value-added activities, on the other hand, don't add value from the customer's perspective and often represent waste."

Exercise 1: Identifying Value-Added Activities

"Let's start by identifying value-added activities in our processes," Sarah instructed. "Each group, revisit your Value Stream Maps and highlight steps that directly contribute to customer value."

Raj Patel's group focused on the assembly process. "Value-added activities include assembling components, conducting quality checks, and packaging," Raj noted. "These steps ensure our product meets customer expectations."

Maria Gonzalez's group worked on the supply chain process. "Ordering supplies, receiving shipments, and managing inventory are value-added," Maria said. "These activities ensure we have the necessary materials to produce our products."

Lisa Chen's group reviewed the customer service workflow. "Responding to customer inquiries, processing returns, and providing technical support are value-added," Lisa pointed out. "These activities directly impact customer satisfaction."

Exercise 2: Identifying Non-Value-Added Activities

"Next, let's identify non-value-added activities," James said. "Look for steps that don't add direct value from the customer's perspective and highlight them."

Raj's group found several non-value-added activities in the assembly process. "We have a lot of waiting time between stages," Raj observed. "And there are multiple instances of rework due to defects."

Maria's group identified inefficiencies in the supply chain. "There's a lot of excess inventory just sitting in storage," Maria said. "And we have redundant paperwork that slows things down."

Lisa's group noted non-value-added activities in customer service. "There's a lot of back-and-forth between departments," Lisa noted. "And we have manual data entry that could be automated."

Discussion: Eliminating Non-Value-Added Activities

Sarah reconvened the group. "Great job identifying these activities. Now, let's discuss how we can eliminate or reduce non-value-added activities."

Raj suggested, "For the waiting times in assembly, we

could implement a more synchronized workflow to minimize delays."

Maria proposed, "To tackle excess inventory, we should adopt Just-in-Time delivery from our suppliers, reducing the need for large stockpiles."

Lisa added, "Automating manual data entry and improving inter-department communication can significantly reduce back-and-forth in customer service."

James encouraged the discussion. "These are excellent suggestions. Eliminating non-value-added activities not only improves efficiency but also enhances the overall value delivered to our customers."

Exercise 3: Creating an Action Plan

"Let's create an action plan to address these non-value-added activities," Sarah instructed. "Each group, list specific actions you will take to streamline your processes."

Raj's group listed their actions:

1. Implement synchronized workflows to reduce waiting times.
2. Integrate quality checks into the assembly line to minimize rework.
3. Use visual management tools to track progress and identify bottlenecks.

Maria's group outlined their plan:

1. Negotiate Just-in-Time delivery agreements with suppliers.
2. Upgrade the inventory management system to reduce excess stock.

3. Simplify paperwork by digitizing forms and using automated tracking.

Lisa's group detailed their steps:

1. Automate routine data entry tasks.
2. Implement a centralized communication platform for customer service.
3. Train staff on efficient problem-solving techniques to reduce back-and-forth.

Conclusion: Focusing on Value

Sarah concluded the session. "By focusing on value-added activities and eliminating waste, we can streamline our processes and deliver greater value to our customers. This is a critical part of our Lean journey."

James added, "Remember, this is an ongoing process. We need to continually evaluate our activities and strive for continuous improvement."

The team left the meeting room energized and committed to implementing their action plans. Aurora Electronics was making significant strides in their Lean transformation, focused on maximizing value and minimizing waste.

Tools for Identifying Value

The Aurora Electronics team gathered in the training room, which had been transformed into a "Lean Toolbox Workshop." The tables were set up with laptops, flip charts, and an array of colorful sticky notes. Sarah Mitchell and James Thompson stood at the front, ready to introduce the tools essential for

CHAPTER 2: IDENTIFYING VALUE

identifying value.

Sarah began, "Welcome to the Lean Toolbox Workshop. Today, we'll explore the tools that help us identify value and streamline our processes. These tools are fundamental to our Lean journey."

James clicked to a slide titled "Tools for Identifying Value." He explained, "We'll cover several key tools: SIPOC Diagrams, the Voice of the Customer, Value Stream Mapping, and the 5 Whys. These tools will help us gain a deeper understanding of our processes and customer needs."

Tool 1: SIPOC Diagrams

"Let's start with SIPOC Diagrams," Sarah said. "SIPOC stands for Suppliers, Inputs, Process, Outputs, and Customers. It's a high-level view of our processes."

Raj Patel's group was tasked with creating a SIPOC Diagram for the assembly process. Raj started, "Our suppliers provide components, the inputs are these components, the process is assembly, the outputs are finished products, and the customers are end users."

The team worked together, listing out each element on a flip chart. They identified key suppliers, critical inputs, major process steps, outputs, and customer segments. This exercise provided a clear overview of the assembly process and its key components.

Tool 2: Voice of the Customer (VoC)

Next, James introduced the Voice of the Customer. "VoC is about capturing customer expectations, preferences, and aversions. It helps us understand what our customers truly value."

Lisa Chen's group conducted a VoC exercise. They reviewed customer feedback from surveys, social media, and direct interactions. "Customers frequently mention the importance of product reliability and timely support," Lisa noted. "They also value innovative features that make our products stand out."

The group listed these customer insights on sticky notes and grouped them by themes. This visual representation helped them see patterns and prioritize customer needs.

Tool 3: Value Stream Mapping (VSM)

"We've already touched on Value Stream Mapping," Sarah said. "Let's take a deeper dive into how it can be used to identify value."

Maria Gonzalez's group revisited their previous VSM exercise, focusing on the supply chain process. "We identified several areas of waste," Maria recalled. "Now, let's use VSM to explore how we can add more value."

The group mapped out the future state, incorporating customer feedback from the VoC exercise. They brainstormed ways to enhance the supply chain, such as implementing more efficient logistics and improving supplier communication.

Tool 4: The 5 Whys

Finally, James introduced the 5 Whys. "The 5 Whys is a problem-solving tool that helps us identify the root cause of issues by repeatedly asking 'Why?'"

Raj's group tackled a recurring issue: frequent defects in the final product. "Why are there defects in the final product?" Raj asked.

"Because some components are faulty," a team member replied.

"Why are the components faulty?" Raj continued.

"Because they are not tested thoroughly before assembly."

"Why are they not tested thoroughly?"

"Because our testing process is outdated and inefficient."
"Why is the testing process outdated?"
"Because we haven't invested in new testing equipment."
"Why haven't we invested in new testing equipment?"
"Because it wasn't prioritized in the budget."

The team identified the root cause: outdated testing equipment. They realized that investing in modern testing tools could significantly reduce defects.

Discussion: Integrating Tools into Daily Operations

Sarah reconvened the group. "These tools are powerful on their own, but even more effective when used together. How can we integrate them into our daily operations?"

Raj suggested, "We should make SIPOC diagrams a standard part of our project planning. It ensures everyone understands the process at a high level."

Lisa added, "Regular VoC exercises can keep us aligned with customer needs. We can incorporate customer feedback into our product development cycles."

Maria proposed, "Using VSM continuously will help us identify and eliminate waste. It should be a living document that we update regularly."

James concluded, "And the 5 Whys should be part of our problem-solving culture. Whenever we face issues, digging deep to find the root cause will help us implement effective solutions."

Action Plan: Embedding Tools into Culture

Sarah outlined the next steps. "To embed these tools into our culture, we need training and regular practice. We'll schedule workshops and create a repository of resources. Each department will appoint a Lean Champion to lead these efforts."

James added, "We'll also set up a Lean Tools Dashboard to track progress and share successes. By integrating these tools into our daily operations, we'll continuously improve and deliver greater value to our customers."

The team left the workshop equipped with practical tools and a clear action plan. Aurora Electronics was now ready to fully embrace Lean principles, with a toolbox that would drive their journey towards operational excellence and customer-centric value delivery.

Aligning Value with Business Goals

The conference room at Aurora Electronics was set up for a strategic alignment meeting. The senior management team, including Sarah Mitchell and James Thompson, gathered around a large table with their laptops open, charts displayed on screens, and a whiteboard ready for notes. This was a critical session aimed at aligning customer value with the company's overarching business goals.

Sarah began, "Today's objective is to ensure that the value we deliver to our customers aligns with our business goals. This alignment is crucial for our success and sustainability."

James added, "We'll review our current business goals, discuss how our customer value propositions fit into these goals, and identify any gaps. Let's start with a recap of our key business goals."

Reviewing Business Goals

Raj Patel, the production manager, summarized the goals. "Our primary business goals include increasing market share, improving operational efficiency, enhancing product innovation, and ensuring customer satisfaction."

Maria Gonzalez, from supply chain management, added, "And we aim to reduce costs and increase profitability while maintaining high standards of quality and reliability."

Lisa Chen, the HR director, noted, "We also want to foster a culture of continuous improvement and employee engagement."

Connecting Value to Goals

Sarah continued, "Let's discuss how the value we identified in our previous sessions connects to these business goals. For instance, improving product reliability directly impacts customer satisfaction and operational efficiency."

Raj's group focused on product assembly. "By ensuring high-quality assembly processes and reducing defects, we align with the goal of improving operational efficiency and customer satisfaction," Raj said. "Reliable products also help increase market share as satisfied customers are more likely to recommend us."

Maria's group connected supply chain improvements to business goals. "Implementing Just-in-Time delivery and enhancing supplier relationships reduce costs and improve efficiency," Maria noted. "This not only increases profitability but also supports innovation by allowing us to be more agile in responding to market demands."

Lisa's group linked customer service enhancements to business goals. "Streamlining our customer service process ensures quicker response times and better support," Lisa explained. "This boosts customer satisfaction and loyalty, which are key to increasing market share."

Identifying Gaps and Opportunities

James took over. "Now, let's identify any gaps where our current processes or value propositions might not fully align with our business goals. Are there areas we need to improve or new opportunities to explore?"

Raj pointed out, "We've identified that investing in modern testing equipment is crucial for reducing defects. This directly supports our goals of improving quality and efficiency."

Maria added, "We also need to leverage technology more effectively in our supply chain to better track shipments and manage inventory. This aligns with our goals of reducing costs and increasing profitability."

Lisa suggested, "In terms of customer service, we can explore new technologies for better communication and problem resolution, further enhancing customer satisfaction and engagement."

Strategic Initiatives

Sarah facilitated a brainstorming session. "Let's create specific strategic initiatives that address these gaps and leverage our opportunities. These initiatives should be actionable and measurable."

Raj's group proposed:

1. Investing in advanced testing equipment to ensure product quality.
2. Implementing synchronized workflows to reduce assembly time and defects.

Maria's group outlined:

1. Upgrading the inventory management system for real-time tracking.
2. Establishing stronger partnerships with key suppliers to improve Just-in-Time delivery.

Lisa's group recommended:

1. Automating routine customer service tasks to improve response times.
2. Training staff in new customer service technologies and techniques.

Action Plan and Metrics

James wrapped up the session by discussing metrics. "We need to establish metrics to measure the success of these initiatives. For example, we can track defect rates, customer satisfaction scores, and inventory turnover rates."

Sarah added, "Each department should set specific, measurable goals related to these initiatives. We'll review progress regularly and adjust our strategies as needed."

Conclusion: Ensuring Alignment

Sarah concluded the meeting. "Aligning customer value with our business goals is essential for our long-term success. By focusing on the initiatives we've outlined, we can ensure that our efforts are driving us toward our goals."

James nodded, "This alignment will not only enhance our operational efficiency and profitability but also ensure that we're consistently delivering value to our customers. Let's stay committed to these initiatives and continue working towards our vision."

The team left the meeting room with a clear understanding of how their daily efforts aligned with the broader business goals. Aurora Electronics was now positioned to drive forward with a cohesive strategy that linked customer value to sustainable business success.

Case Studies: Value Identification in Practice

The Aurora Electronics team gathered in a modern meeting room, the walls adorned with charts and timelines of previous projects. Sarah Mitchell and James Thompson stood by a projector, ready to share real-world examples of how value identification had driven success in various companies. This session aimed to learn from others' experiences and apply those lessons to their own Lean journey.

Sarah began, "Today, we'll look at case studies of companies that have successfully identified and delivered value through Lean principles. These examples will provide insights into practical applications and inspire our efforts."

James added, "We'll discuss each case study, identify key takeaways, and brainstorm how we can apply these lessons to Aurora Electronics."

Case Study 1: Toyota Production System

Sarah clicked to the first slide showing Toyota's logo. "Our first case study is Toyota, the pioneer of Lean manufacturing. Toyota's success is built on its relentless focus on eliminating waste and improving value."

Raj Patel shared his insights. "Toyota's Just-in-Time production system is legendary. They only produce what is needed, when it's needed, and in the amount needed. This reduces inventory costs and ensures high-quality products."

Sarah nodded. "Exactly. Toyota's focus on continuous improvement and respect for people has also been critical. They empower employees to identify waste and suggest improvements, creating a culture of ongoing value enhancement."

The team discussed how they could implement similar

practices. "We should empower our assembly line workers to identify inefficiencies and suggest changes," Raj suggested. "And adopting a more rigorous Just-in-Time inventory system could reduce our overheads."

Case Study 2: Dell's Direct-to-Consumer Model

James introduced the next case study. "Dell revolutionized the computer industry with its direct-to-consumer model. By cutting out intermediaries, Dell was able to offer customized products and respond quickly to customer demands."

Maria Gonzalez explained, "Dell's approach to inventory management is another key takeaway. They maintained minimal inventory, reducing costs and avoiding obsolescence. This model allowed them to pass savings onto customers and deliver value."

Lisa Chen added, "Their focus on customer feedback was also crucial. Dell used VoC methods to understand what customers wanted and adapted their offerings accordingly."

The team brainstormed applications for Aurora Electronics. "We could improve our customization options and streamline our supply chain to be more responsive to market changes," Maria suggested. "And enhancing our customer feedback loop will help us stay aligned with customer needs."

Case Study 3: Amazon's Customer Obsession

Sarah clicked to the next slide, featuring Amazon's logo. "Amazon's success is rooted in its relentless focus on customer satisfaction. Their principle of 'customer obsession' drives every aspect of their business."

Lisa shared her thoughts. "Amazon uses data extensively to understand customer behavior and preferences. They constantly refine their processes to enhance the customer experience, from fast delivery times to personalized recommendations."

James added, "Amazon's use of technology, such as automation in warehouses and advanced analytics, has also been pivotal. They've significantly reduced operational costs while improving service quality."

The team discussed potential implementations. "We can leverage data analytics to better understand our customers and streamline our operations," Lisa suggested. "And investing in automation could enhance our efficiency and reduce costs."

Case Study 4: Starbucks' Lean Transformation

James introduced the next case study. "Starbucks applied Lean principles to their stores to improve service speed and quality. They focused on value stream mapping and eliminating waste from their processes."

Raj highlighted key points. "Starbucks identified bottlenecks in their service process, such as long waiting times and inefficient workflows. By addressing these issues, they enhanced the customer experience and increased throughput."

Sarah added, "They also empowered employees to take part in the improvement process, fostering a culture of continuous improvement and engagement."

The team brainstormed ideas for Aurora Electronics. "We can conduct value stream mapping in our customer service department to identify and eliminate bottlenecks," Raj suggested. "And involving our employees in the process will ensure buy-in and innovative solutions."

Case Study 5: The Boeing Production System

Sarah presented the final case study. "Boeing applied Lean principles to their manufacturing processes, particularly in the production of the 737 aircraft. They focused on reducing lead times and improving quality."

Maria explained, "Boeing used techniques like cellular manufacturing and visual management to streamline their processes. These changes significantly reduced production times and improved product quality."

James added, "They also emphasized supplier collaboration, ensuring that their entire supply chain was aligned with Lean principles."

The team discussed how these lessons could apply to Aurora Electronics. "We should explore cellular manufacturing techniques to improve our assembly process," Maria suggested. "And enhancing our supplier relationships will help us achieve better alignment and efficiency."

Conclusion: Applying Lessons Learned

Sarah wrapped up the session. "These case studies provide valuable insights into how companies across various industries have successfully identified and delivered value through Lean principles. Let's use these lessons to inform our strategies."

James added, "Our next steps involve creating action plans based on these insights. We'll assign teams to focus on specific initiatives, such as enhancing our inventory management, leveraging data analytics, and improving customer feedback loops."

The team left the meeting room inspired and equipped with new ideas. By learning from the successes of others, Aurora Electronics was ready to take their Lean journey to the next level, ensuring that their efforts were aligned with delivering maximum value to their customers and achieving their business goals.

3

Chapter 3: Value Stream Mapping

Basics of Value Stream Mapping

The Aurora Electronics team assembled in their largest conference room, which was set up for a comprehensive training session on Value Stream Mapping (VSM). The walls were lined with whiteboards, and tables were equipped with markers, sticky notes, and large sheets of paper. Sarah Mitchell and James Thompson stood at the front, ready to introduce the team to the basics of VSM.

Sarah began with a warm smile, "Welcome, everyone. Today's session is all about Value Stream Mapping. VSM is a critical tool in Lean management, helping us visualize and improve our processes."

James added, "We'll start with the basics of VSM, including its purpose, key components, and how to create a value stream map. Let's dive in."

Introduction to Value Stream Mapping

Sarah started with an overview. "Value Stream Mapping

CHAPTER 3: VALUE STREAM MAPPING

is a Lean tool that helps us visualize the flow of materials and information as a product makes its way through the value stream. It allows us to see both the current state and future state of our processes, helping us identify waste and opportunities for improvement."

James clicked to a slide titled "Components of a Value Stream Map." He explained, "A value stream map typically includes the following components: process steps, information flow, material flow, and key performance metrics."

Exercise: Creating a Simple Value Stream Map

"Let's create a simple value stream map to illustrate the concept," Sarah suggested. "Imagine we're mapping the process of assembling our new XYZ electronic device."

Raj Patel's group was eager to start. They gathered around a large sheet of paper and began listing the main process steps: receiving components, assembling parts, quality inspection, packaging, and shipping.

Maria Gonzalez's group focused on information flow. They used arrows and symbols to indicate how information moved between departments, from order receipt to shipping notifications.

Lisa Chen's group tackled material flow. They drew lines representing the movement of components and finished products through the production line.

Identifying Key Metrics

James highlighted the importance of metrics. "To complete our value stream map, we need to include key performance metrics. These could be cycle time, lead time, inventory levels, and defect rates."

Raj's group discussed cycle times for each process step. "Receiving components takes about two hours, assembly takes six hours, quality inspection takes one hour, packaging takes another hour, and shipping preparation takes two hours," Raj noted.

Maria's group estimated lead times. "From order receipt to shipping, the total lead time is around 24 hours," Maria said.

Lisa's group considered inventory levels and defect rates. "We usually have a day's worth of components in inventory, and our defect rate is currently at 2%," Lisa reported.

Visualizing the Current State

Sarah and James helped the teams consolidate their findings into a comprehensive current state value stream map. They used different colors for process steps, information flow, and material flow, making the map easy to read and understand.

Sarah pointed to the completed map on the whiteboard. "This is our current state value stream map. It provides a clear picture of our process as it stands today, highlighting areas of waste and inefficiencies."

James added, "By visualizing our current state, we can start to see where we have bottlenecks, delays, and non-value-added activities. This is the first step in identifying opportunities for improvement."

Discussion: Analyzing the Current State

The team gathered around the map, discussing their observations.

Raj noted, "We have a significant delay in the assembly process. It takes longer than any other step and could be a bottleneck."

Maria pointed out, "There's a lot of waiting time between receiving components and starting assembly. Maybe we can streamline the handoff."

Lisa observed, "Our defect rate, though not terrible, still

indicates room for improvement, especially in the quality inspection stage."

Creating a Future State Map

Sarah guided the next exercise. "Let's imagine our ideal process and create a future state value stream map. Think about ways to eliminate waste, reduce cycle times, and improve quality."

Raj's group suggested automating part of the assembly process to reduce cycle time. "If we automate some of the more repetitive tasks, we could cut assembly time in half," Raj proposed.

Maria's group recommended improving communication between departments. "Implementing a real-time tracking system could reduce waiting times and ensure a smoother flow of materials," Maria said.

Lisa's group focused on enhancing quality control. "Investing in better inspection tools and training could lower our defect rate," Lisa suggested.

The team worked together to draw their future state map, incorporating these improvements. The new map showed a streamlined process with reduced cycle times, better information flow, and improved quality metrics.

Conclusion: Implementing and Iterating

James concluded the session. "Creating a future state value stream map is just the beginning. The next steps involve implementing these changes and continuously iterating based on new data and feedback."

Sarah added, "Remember, VSM is a dynamic tool. As we implement improvements, we'll revisit our maps, measure our progress, and make further adjustments. This ongoing process of improvement is at the heart of Lean management."

The team left the training room energized and equipped with a powerful new tool. Aurora Electronics was now ready to apply Value Stream Mapping to their operations, driving continuous improvement and operational excellence.

Steps to Create a Value Stream Map

The Aurora Electronics team reconvened in the workshop room, ready to learn and practice the detailed steps of creating a Value Stream Map (VSM). The atmosphere was a mix of anticipation and focus as Sarah Mitchell and James Thompson prepared to guide them through a hands-on session.

Sarah began, "Welcome back. Today, we're going to dive deeper into the steps required to create a Value Stream Map. We'll follow a structured approach to ensure we capture all the necessary details."

James added, "We'll be mapping out the assembly process for our flagship product, the XYZ electronic device. Let's get started."

Step 1: Define the Scope and Boundaries

Sarah initiated the first step. "The first step is to define the scope and boundaries of your value stream. For our exercise, we'll focus on the assembly process from receiving components to shipping the finished product."

Raj Patel's group quickly outlined the boundaries on a large sheet of paper. They identified the starting point as the receiving dock and the endpoint as the shipping department.

Step 2: Map the Current State

James explained the importance of the current state map. "Next, we need to map the current state. This involves detailing all the steps, information flows, and material movements as they currently exist."

The team split into smaller groups, each tasked with a specific part of the process.

Raj's group began with receiving components. They listed each action: unloading trucks, inspecting components, and storing them in inventory.

Maria Gonzalez's group focused on the assembly line. They noted each step: picking components, assembling parts, quality checks, and moving completed units to packaging.

Lisa Chen's group handled the final stages: packaging the products, labeling them, and preparing them for shipment.

Step 3: Identify Process Data

Sarah highlighted the need for process data. "We need to collect data for each process step. This includes cycle time, lead time, and inventory levels."

Raj's group timed how long it took to unload and inspect components, noting it took about two hours.

Maria's group recorded the assembly time for each unit, which was approximately six hours, including quality checks.

Lisa's group measured the time taken for packaging and labeling, which was around one hour.

Step 4: Create the Current State Map

James guided the team in consolidating their findings. "Now, let's bring it all together and create the current state map. Use symbols to represent different elements like process steps, inventory, and information flow."

The groups collaborated, drawing symbols for each process step and connecting them with arrows to indicate material and information flow. They added data boxes to each step, showing cycle times, lead times, and inventory levels.

Raj pointed out, "We have significant waiting times between

receiving components and starting assembly. This is a clear area for improvement."

Step 5: Analyze the Current State

Sarah emphasized the analysis phase. "With the current state map complete, we need to analyze it for waste and inefficiencies. Look for delays, bottlenecks, and non-value-added activities."

Maria's group identified the assembly process as a bottleneck. "It's the longest part of the process and often creates delays downstream," Maria noted.

Lisa's group found excessive inventory levels between assembly and packaging. "We're holding too many finished units before packaging, which ties up capital," Lisa explained.

Step 6: Design the Future State

James moved the discussion forward. "The next step is to design the future state map. This involves envisioning an ideal process with reduced waste and improved efficiency."

The team brainstormed improvements. Raj suggested, "We can streamline the receiving process by implementing more efficient inspection methods."

Maria proposed automating part of the assembly line to speed up production. "Automating repetitive tasks could halve our assembly time," she said.

Lisa recommended a just-in-time approach to packaging. "We should aim to package units as soon as they come off the assembly line to reduce inventory," she suggested.

Step 7: Implement the Future State

Sarah concluded with implementation. "Finally, we need to implement the future state map. This involves setting clear goals, assigning responsibilities, and tracking progress."

The team created an action plan. Raj's group would pilot

the new inspection methods, Maria's group would oversee the assembly line automation, and Lisa's group would implement the just-in-time packaging system.

James added, "We'll set up regular review meetings to track our progress and make adjustments as needed."

Conclusion: Continuous Improvement

Sarah wrapped up the session. "Remember, Value Stream Mapping is a continuous improvement tool. As we implement these changes, we'll revisit our maps, measure our progress, and refine our processes."

James nodded, "By following these steps, we can ensure that our value stream maps accurately reflect our processes and guide us toward greater efficiency and value."

The team left the workshop with a clear understanding of the steps involved in creating a Value Stream Map and a concrete plan to enhance their assembly process. Aurora Electronics was now well-equipped to drive continuous improvement and operational excellence through effective value stream mapping.

Identifying Waste in the Value Stream

The Aurora Electronics team gathered in the workshop room, energized from their previous sessions on Value Stream Mapping (VSM). Large sheets of paper covered the walls, each displaying the current state maps they had created. Sarah Mitchell and James Thompson were ready to guide them through the next crucial step: identifying waste in the value stream.

Sarah started, "Good morning, everyone. Today, we're going to focus on identifying waste in our value stream. This is a critical step in Lean management because eliminating waste allows us to increase efficiency and add more value."

James added, "We'll review the seven types of waste and apply these concepts to our current state maps. Let's get started."

Introduction to the Seven Types of Waste

Sarah clicked to a slide listing the seven types of waste. "In Lean, waste is anything that doesn't add value to the customer. The seven types of waste are: Transportation, Inventory, Motion, Waiting, Overproduction, Overprocessing, and Defects."

James elaborated on each type, "For example, transportation waste involves unnecessary movement of materials, while waiting waste refers to idle time when nothing is being produced."

Step 1: Review the Current State Map

The team divided into their smaller groups, each reviewing the current state maps they had created.

Raj Patel's group focused on the receiving and initial inspection process. Maria Gonzalez's group examined the assembly line, and Lisa Chen's group reviewed the packaging and shipping stages.

Step 2: Identify Waste in Each Process Step

Sarah and James moved between groups, encouraging them to look critically at each process step.

Raj's group identified waiting waste. "There's a lot of idle time between receiving components and starting assembly," Raj noted. "Components sit in inventory for too long."

Maria's group found motion waste. "Our workers move back and forth across the assembly line multiple times for each unit," Maria pointed out. "We need to reconfigure the line to reduce unnecessary movement."

Lisa's group highlighted overproduction waste. "We often package more units than we can ship in a day, leading to excess finished goods inventory," Lisa explained.

Step 3: Use Sticky Notes to Mark Waste

James handed out colored sticky notes. "Use these to mark each type of waste on your maps. This visual representation will help us clearly see where waste is occurring."

Raj's group used yellow notes for waiting waste, marking areas where components sat idle. Maria's group used blue notes for motion waste, placing them along paths of unnecessary movement. Lisa's group used red notes for overproduction waste, marking the excess inventory areas.

Step 4: Discuss and Analyze Identified Waste

Sarah called for a group discussion. "Let's analyze the waste we've identified. What patterns do you see? How does this waste impact our efficiency and customer value?"

Raj observed, "The waiting waste in our receiving process delays the entire production schedule. We need to streamline this step to keep the flow moving."

Maria noted, "The motion waste on the assembly line slows down production and leads to worker fatigue. A more efficient layout will reduce these issues."

Lisa added, "Our overproduction leads to high inventory costs and risks of obsolescence. We need to align our packaging more closely with shipping schedules."

Step 5: Prioritize Waste for Elimination

James emphasized prioritization. "Now, let's prioritize the waste areas for elimination. Focus on the wastes that have the most significant impact on our efficiency and customer value."

Raj's group decided to tackle waiting waste first. "Reducing idle time will have an immediate positive impact on our lead time," Raj suggested.

Maria's group prioritized motion waste. "Reconfiguring the assembly line layout is a big project, but it will greatly improve our efficiency," Maria said.

Lisa's group focused on overproduction waste. "Aligning packaging with shipping schedules will reduce costs and improve cash flow," Lisa noted.

Step 6: Develop Action Plans for Waste Elimination

Sarah guided the next step. "Let's develop action plans to eliminate the prioritized wastes. Outline specific actions, assign responsibilities, and set timelines."

Raj's group planned to implement a kanban system in the receiving area to reduce waiting time. "This will ensure components move directly into production as needed," Raj explained.

Maria's group proposed a new assembly line layout with designated stations and ergonomic designs. "We'll pilot this layout in one section before rolling it out fully," Maria suggested.

Lisa's group decided to synchronize packaging with real-time sales data. "We'll use data analytics to adjust packaging schedules based on actual demand," Lisa said.

Step 7: Implement and Monitor Changes

James concluded with implementation. "Implement your action plans and monitor the results. Use metrics to track improvements and make adjustments as needed."

Sarah added, "We'll review progress in our weekly Lean meetings. This iterative process will help us continuously improve."

Conclusion: Embedding Waste Elimination in Culture

Sarah wrapped up the session. "Identifying and eliminating waste is an ongoing process. By embedding this mindset in our culture, we'll drive continuous improvement and operational excellence."

James nodded, "Remember, every small improvement adds up. Let's stay committed to identifying and eliminating waste to enhance our value stream."

The team left the workshop with a clear understanding of the types of waste and concrete plans to eliminate them. Aurora Electronics was now equipped to refine their processes further, ensuring they operated as efficiently and effectively as possible.

Using Value Stream Maps for Continuous Improvement

The Aurora Electronics team gathered in the strategy room for their weekly continuous improvement meeting. Large screens displayed the current state and future state value stream maps, along with charts showing key performance metrics. Sarah Mitchell and James Thompson led the discussion, ready to guide the team through their journey of ongoing improvement using value stream maps.

Sarah began, "Welcome, everyone. Today, we're going to focus on how we can use value stream maps for continuous improvement. Our goal is to ensure that we're always striving for greater efficiency and value."

James added, "We'll review our progress, identify areas for further improvement, and develop action plans to drive positive change. Let's dive in."

Reviewing Progress

The team started by reviewing their progress since the

last meeting. They examined the key performance metrics, comparing them to their targets and discussing any deviations.

Raj Patel's group reported on the implementation of the kanban system in the receiving area. "We've seen a significant reduction in waiting time for components, which has helped us maintain a smoother production flow," Raj said.

Maria Gonzalez's group shared updates on the new assembly line layout. "The redesigned layout has reduced motion waste and improved worker efficiency," Maria explained.

Lisa Chen's group discussed the synchronization of packaging with real-time sales data. "By adjusting our packaging schedules based on actual demand, we've been able to reduce overproduction and optimize inventory levels," Lisa reported.

Identifying Areas for Further Improvement

Sarah prompted the team to identify areas for further improvement based on their current state maps and performance data.

Raj's group highlighted a bottleneck they had identified in the assembly process. "Despite the layout changes, we still have a bottleneck at the quality inspection station. We need to find ways to speed up this process," Raj suggested.

Maria's group noted inefficiencies in material flow between assembly stations. "There are still instances where workers need to backtrack or wait for components, causing delays," Maria pointed out.

Lisa's group raised concerns about variability in shipping schedules. "Our packaging adjustments have helped, but we're still experiencing occasional spikes in demand that strain our packaging capacity," Lisa said.

Developing Action Plans

James guided the team in developing action plans to address

the identified areas for improvement.

Raj's group proposed cross-training workers to perform quality inspections. "By having multiple workers trained in quality inspection, we can ensure that there's always someone available to keep the process moving," Raj suggested.

Maria's group recommended implementing visual cues and standard operating procedures to streamline material flow. "Clear signage and standardized procedures will reduce confusion and minimize delays," Maria proposed.

Lisa's group suggested investing in additional packaging equipment to handle peak demand periods. "Having backup equipment will allow us to quickly scale up our packaging capacity when needed," Lisa said.

Committing to Continuous Improvement

Sarah emphasized the importance of commitment to continuous improvement. "Continuous improvement is not a one-time effort; it's an ongoing commitment to excellence. Let's stay focused on identifying opportunities, implementing solutions, and measuring our progress."

James nodded in agreement. "By using value stream maps as our guide, we can ensure that every improvement we make is aligned with our goals of efficiency, quality, and customer satisfaction."

Conclusion: Driving Operational Excellence

Sarah concluded the meeting with a note of encouragement. "As we continue on our Lean journey, let's remember that every improvement, no matter how small, brings us closer to our vision of operational excellence. Together, we can build a culture of continuous improvement that propels us toward success."

The team left the meeting room with renewed determination, armed with action plans to drive further improvements in their value stream. Aurora Electronics was well on its way to achieving its goals of efficiency, quality, and customer satisfaction through the power of continuous improvement.

Case Studies: Successful Value Stream Mapping

The Aurora Electronics leadership team gathered in the boardroom for a special presentation on successful Value Stream Mapping (VSM) case studies. Sarah Mitchell and James Thompson stood at the front, ready to share real-world examples of how VSM had driven positive change in various organizations.

Sarah began, "Good afternoon, everyone. Today, we'll be discussing case studies of companies that have successfully used Value Stream Mapping to drive improvement and achieve operational excellence."

James added, "These case studies will provide valuable insights and inspiration as we continue our own Lean journey. Let's dive in."

Case Study 1: Toyota Production System

Sarah clicked to the first slide, displaying Toyota's logo. "Our first case study is the Toyota Production System, known for its pioneering use of Lean principles. Toyota's success is built on their commitment to continuous improvement and waste reduction."

James elaborated, "Through Value Stream Mapping, Toyota identified and eliminated waste in their production processes, resulting in shorter lead times, lower costs, and higher quality."

Case Study 2: Starbucks' Lean Transformation

Sarah switched to the next slide, featuring the Starbucks

logo. "Starbucks applied Lean principles to their store operations, streamlining processes to improve service speed and quality."

James explained, "Value Stream Mapping helped Starbucks identify bottlenecks in their service flow, leading to changes in layout and staffing that reduced wait times and enhanced the customer experience."

Case Study 3: Amazon's Fulfillment Centers

The next slide displayed the Amazon logo. "Amazon's fulfillment centers are a prime example of efficient operations driven by Lean principles," Sarah said.

James continued, "By using Value Stream Mapping to optimize their processes, Amazon has been able to fulfill orders quickly and accurately, meeting customer expectations and maintaining their position as a market leader."

Case Study 4: GE Healthcare's Radiology Services

Sarah moved on to the next slide, featuring the GE Healthcare logo. "GE Healthcare applied Value Stream Mapping to their radiology services, aiming to improve patient care and efficiency."

James shared, "Through VSM, GE Healthcare identified opportunities to reduce wait times for patients and streamline the diagnostic process. This resulted in faster diagnoses, improved patient satisfaction, and increased throughput for the facility."

Case Study 5: Ford Motor Company

The final slide displayed the Ford logo. "Ford Motor Company utilized Value Stream Mapping to enhance their manufacturing processes and increase competitiveness," Sarah explained.

James concluded, "By mapping their value streams, Ford

identified inefficiencies and implemented changes that improved production efficiency, reduced costs, and enhanced product quality, leading to greater customer satisfaction."

Discussion and Application

Sarah opened the floor for discussion. "These case studies demonstrate the power of Value Stream Mapping in driving operational excellence. Let's discuss how we can apply these lessons to our own operations at Aurora Electronics."

The team engaged in a lively discussion, drawing parallels between the case studies and their own challenges and opportunities. They brainstormed ideas for applying VSM to their assembly processes, supply chain management, and customer service operations.

Conclusion: Driving Success Through VSM

James wrapped up the presentation. "By learning from these successful case studies and applying the principles of Value Stream Mapping to our own operations, we can drive positive change, improve efficiency, and achieve our goals of operational excellence."

Sarah nodded in agreement. "Let's use these insights to guide our Lean journey and ensure that every action we take adds value to our customers and contributes to the success of Aurora Electronics."

The team left the boardroom inspired and motivated, ready to apply the lessons learned from the case studies to their own value stream mapping efforts. With a clear understanding of the power of VSM, Aurora Electronics was well-positioned to drive success and innovation in their operations.

Tools and Software for Value Stream Mapping

The Aurora Electronics team gathered in the training room for a demonstration of tools and software used for Value Stream Mapping (VSM). Sarah Mitchell and James Thompson stood at the front, ready to showcase the latest technologies that could enhance their VSM efforts.

Sarah began, "Good morning, everyone. Today, we'll be exploring the various tools and software available to aid us in our Value Stream Mapping efforts. These tools can streamline the process, improve collaboration, and provide valuable insights into our operations."

James added, "Let's dive in and see how these tools can help us drive continuous improvement and achieve operational excellence."

Demonstration of Physical Mapping Tools

Sarah showcased physical mapping tools such as large sheets of paper, sticky notes, and markers. "These traditional tools are simple yet effective for creating value stream maps. They allow for hands-on collaboration and can be easily modified as needed."

James demonstrated how to use sticky notes to represent process steps, arrows to indicate material and information flow, and data boxes to capture key metrics. "Physical mapping tools provide a tangible representation of our value streams, making it easy for everyone to understand and contribute."

Introduction to VSM Software

Sarah introduced VSM software as a digital alternative to physical mapping tools. "VSM software offers additional features such as real-time collaboration, data analysis, and visualization tools that can enhance our VSM efforts."

James showcased a popular VSM software package, demonstrating how to create digital value stream maps, input process data, and analyze metrics. "With VSM software, we can create, share, and iterate on our value stream maps more efficiently, leading to quicker insights and improvements."

Integration with Lean Management Systems

Sarah highlighted the importance of integrating VSM software with broader Lean management systems. "Many VSM software packages offer integration with other Lean tools and methodologies, allowing for a more holistic approach to continuous improvement."

James demonstrated how VSM software could be integrated with tools such as kanban boards, root cause analysis software, and project management platforms. "By integrating VSM software with our existing Lean management systems, we can create a seamless workflow that supports our Lean initiatives from start to finish."

Customization and Scalability

Sarah emphasized the importance of choosing VSM tools that are customizable and scalable to meet the unique needs of Aurora Electronics. "Look for tools that allow for customization of templates, workflows, and metrics to ensure that they align with our specific goals and processes."

James showcased how VSM software could be customized to include company-specific process steps, metrics, and visualizations. "By tailoring our VSM tools to fit our unique requirements, we can ensure that they provide maximum value and support our continuous improvement efforts effectively."

Conclusion: Leveraging Technology for Success

Sarah concluded the demonstration by encouraging the team to leverage technology to drive success in their VSM efforts. "By embracing tools and software for Value Stream Mapping, we can streamline our processes, improve collaboration, and drive continuous improvement more effectively than ever before."

James nodded in agreement. "Let's explore these tools further and see how they can support our Lean journey toward operational excellence."

The team left the training room excited to explore the new tools and software available for Value Stream Mapping. With a clear understanding of their capabilities and benefits, Aurora Electronics was well-equipped to leverage technology to drive success and innovation in their continuous improvement efforts.

4

Chapter 4: Eliminating Waste

The Seven Types of Waste (Muda)

The Aurora Electronics team gathered in the workshop room for a training session on eliminating waste. Sarah Mitchell and James Thompson stood at the front, ready to delve into the seven types of waste, known as Muda in Lean terminology.

Sarah began, "Good morning, everyone. Today, we're going to focus on one of the core principles of Lean management: eliminating waste. Waste, or Muda, is anything that doesn't add value to our customers or our business. By identifying and eliminating waste, we can streamline our processes and improve efficiency."

James added, "There are seven types of waste in Lean: Transportation, Inventory, Motion, Waiting, Overproduction, Overprocessing, and Defects. Let's explore each type in detail and see how they manifest in our operations."

Type 1: Transportation Waste

Sarah explained, "Transportation waste occurs when we move materials or products more than necessary. This includes unnecessary movement of goods between processes, facilities, or locations."

James provided examples, "For instance, if we transport components from one end of the factory to the other multiple times during the assembly process, that's transportation waste. It adds time, cost, and the risk of damage without adding any value."

Type 2: Inventory Waste

Sarah continued, "Inventory waste refers to excess inventory that ties up capital, takes up space, and increases the risk of obsolescence or damage."

James elaborated, "Having too much inventory on hand can lead to increased storage costs, delays in production, and difficulties in tracking and managing inventory levels effectively."

Type 3: Motion Waste

Sarah moved on, "Motion waste occurs when workers or equipment move more than necessary to perform a task. This can lead to inefficiency, fatigue, and increased risk of errors or accidents."

James gave an example, "If workers have to repeatedly bend, stretch, or reach for tools or materials during assembly, that's motion waste. It adds strain to the workers and slows down the process."

Type 4: Waiting Waste

Sarah highlighted waiting waste, "Waiting waste occurs when materials, products, or information sit idle, waiting for the next step in the process."

James illustrated, "For example, if workers have to wait for components to arrive before they can start assembly, that's waiting waste. It leads to delays, downtime, and decreased productivity."

Type 5: Overproduction Waste

Sarah continued, "Overproduction waste happens when we produce more than is needed, leading to excess inventory, increased lead times, and higher costs."

James explained, "Producing more units than there is demand for can result in wasted resources, storage space, and money. It also increases the risk of producing defective or obsolete products."

Type 6: Overprocessing Waste

Sarah moved on to overprocessing waste, "Overprocessing waste occurs when we use more resources, time, or effort than necessary to complete a task."

James provided examples, "If we perform additional steps or use higher-quality materials than required by the customer, that's overprocessing waste. It adds unnecessary cost and complexity to the process."

Type 7: Defects Waste

Sarah concluded with defects waste, "Defects waste occurs when products or services don't meet the quality standards, leading to rework, scrap, or customer dissatisfaction."

James emphasized the impact, "Defective products not only result in additional costs for rework or scrap but also damage our reputation and erode customer trust."

Conclusion: Identifying and Eliminating Waste

Sarah wrapped up the session by encouraging the team to actively identify and eliminate the seven types of waste in their operations. "By rooting out waste at its source, we can streamline our processes, improve efficiency, and deliver greater value to our customers and our business."

James nodded in agreement, "Let's work together to eliminate waste and drive continuous improvement in every aspect of our operations."

The team left the training room with a renewed focus on identifying and eliminating waste in their processes. With a clear understanding of the seven types of waste, Aurora Electronics was ready to embark on their journey toward operational excellence through waste elimination.

Techniques for Identifying Waste

The Aurora Electronics team assembled for a Gemba Walk, a hands-on approach to identifying waste in their processes. Led by Sarah Mitchell and James Thompson, they ventured onto the factory floor to observe operations firsthand and identify opportunities for waste reduction.

Sarah began, "Welcome to our Gemba Walk, where we'll observe our processes in action and identify opportunities to eliminate waste. By going to the source, we can gain valuable insights and make informed decisions about improvements."

James added, "Remember to keep an open mind and observe with a critical eye. Let's work together to uncover waste and drive positive change."

Observing Transportation Waste

As they walked through the factory, the team observed the movement of materials and products between workstations. They noted instances where components were transported long distances or moved multiple times during the assembly process.

Sarah pointed out, "Here we see transportation waste

in action. Components are being transported back and forth between workstations, adding unnecessary time and complexity to the process."

James encouraged the team to brainstorm solutions, "How can we reduce this transportation waste? Perhaps by rearranging workstations or implementing a kanban system to control inventory flow."

Identifying Inventory Waste

The team moved to the inventory storage area, where they observed shelves filled with excess components and finished goods. They noted instances of overstocked items and obsolete inventory.

Sarah remarked, "This is a classic example of inventory waste. Excess inventory ties up capital, takes up valuable space, and increases the risk of obsolescence."

James suggested, "We could implement a just-in-time inventory system to reduce excess inventory levels and replenish stock only when needed."

Spotting Motion Waste

As they observed workers on the assembly line, the team noticed repetitive or unnecessary movements. They observed instances where workers had to bend, stretch, or reach for tools or materials.

Sarah pointed out, "This is motion waste in action. Workers are expending unnecessary energy and time on non-value-added activities, leading to inefficiency and fatigue."

James proposed, "We could redesign workstations to optimize ergonomics and minimize unnecessary movement. Providing workers with tools and materials within easy reach can also help reduce motion waste."

Addressing Waiting Waste

In certain areas of the factory, the team observed instances where workers were waiting for materials, instructions, or equipment. They noted delays and idle time that slowed down the production process.

Sarah noted, "Waiting waste is evident here. Idle time leads to lost productivity and delays in meeting customer demand."

James suggested, "We could implement cross-training programs to ensure that workers can perform multiple tasks and fill in for each other during downtimes. Improving communication and coordination between departments can also help minimize waiting waste."

Conclusion: Taking Action

As the Gemba Walk concluded, Sarah and James gathered the team for a debriefing session. They discussed their observations and proposed solutions for eliminating waste in their processes.

Sarah concluded, "By actively observing our processes and identifying waste, we can take targeted action to improve efficiency, reduce costs, and deliver greater value to our customers. Let's continue to leverage Gemba Walks as a tool for continuous improvement."

James nodded in agreement, "Every small improvement we make adds up to significant gains in the long run. Let's stay committed to eliminating waste and driving excellence in everything we do."

The team left the Gemba Walk with a renewed sense of purpose and a commitment to identifying and eliminating waste in their processes. With Gemba Walks as a regular practice, Aurora Electronics was well-positioned to achieve operational excellence through waste reduction.

Tools for Waste Elimination

The Aurora Electronics team gathered in the workshop room, eager to explore tools and techniques for waste elimination. Sarah Mitchell and James Thompson stood at the front, ready to introduce the team to a variety of tools that could help them identify and eliminate waste in their processes.

Sarah began, "Good morning, everyone. Today, we're going to discuss tools and techniques for waste elimination. By leveraging the right tools, we can streamline our processes, improve efficiency, and deliver greater value to our customers."

James added, "Let's explore some of the most effective tools for identifying and eliminating waste in our operations."

Value Stream Mapping

Sarah introduced Value Stream Mapping (VSM) as a powerful tool for identifying waste in processes. "Value Stream Mapping allows us to visualize the flow of materials and information through our processes, making it easier to identify areas of waste and opportunities for improvement."

James demonstrated how to create a value stream map, input process data, and analyze key metrics to identify waste. "By mapping out our value streams, we can pinpoint inefficiencies, such as waiting time, excess inventory, and unnecessary motion, and develop targeted strategies for waste elimination."

5 Whys Analysis

Sarah introduced the 5 Whys analysis technique as a simple yet effective tool for root cause analysis. "The 5 Whys technique involves asking 'why' repeatedly to drill down to the underlying cause of a problem."

James provided an example, "For instance, if we identify a defect in a product, we can ask 'why' it occurred. By asking 'why' five times, we can uncover the root cause, whether it's a faulty machine, inadequate training, or a flawed process."

Kaizen Events

Sarah explained Kaizen events as focused, short-term improvement projects aimed at eliminating waste and improving processes. "Kaizen events bring together cross-functional teams to tackle specific problems and implement rapid improvements."

James showcased examples of past Kaizen events, such as reorganizing workstations for better flow, implementing 5S practices for workplace organization, and standardizing work procedures to reduce variability.

Poka-Yoke (Mistake-Proofing)

Sarah introduced Poka-Yoke as a technique for mistake-proofing processes to prevent defects and errors. "Poka-Yoke involves designing processes or tools in a way that makes errors impossible or easily detectable."

James provided examples, "For instance, using color-coded components to ensure correct assembly, or implementing sensors to detect missing parts before production begins."

Lean Six Sigma

Sarah briefly mentioned Lean Six Sigma as a comprehensive methodology for waste elimination and process improvement. "Lean Six Sigma combines Lean principles with statistical analysis to identify and eliminate waste and variability in processes."

James explained, "By using tools such as DMAIC (Define, Measure, Analyze, Improve, Control), we can systematically improve processes, reduce defects, and increase efficiency."

Conclusion: Empowering Waste Elimination

Sarah concluded the workshop by emphasizing the importance of leveraging these tools and techniques to drive waste elimination and continuous improvement. "By equipping ourselves with the right tools, we can empower our team to identify waste, implement targeted solutions, and achieve operational excellence."

James nodded in agreement, "Let's embrace these tools and techniques as we strive to eliminate waste and deliver greater value to our customers and our business."

The team left the workshop feeling inspired and empowered, armed with new tools and techniques to drive waste elimination and continuous improvement in their processes. With a clear roadmap for action, Aurora Electronics was well-positioned to achieve their goals of operational excellence.

Lean Tools: 5S, Kaizen, and Poka-Yoke

The Aurora Electronics team gathered on the factory floor, ready to implement Lean tools to eliminate waste and drive continuous improvement. Sarah Mitchell and James Thompson led the team as they embarked on a journey to apply 5S, Kaizen, and Poka-Yoke principles to their processes.

Sarah began, "Good afternoon, everyone. Today, we're going to put our Lean tools into action to eliminate waste and improve our processes. By implementing 5S, conducting Kaizen events, and applying Poka-Yoke principles, we can create a workplace that is organized, efficient, and error-free."

James added, "Let's work together to transform our work environment and drive positive change."

Implementing 5S: Sort

The team started with the first step of 5S: Sort. They sorted through their work areas, identifying and removing unnecessary items, tools, and materials.

Sarah explained, "Sorting helps us eliminate clutter and ensure that only essential items are kept in the work area. This reduces waste, improves efficiency, and creates a safer, more organized workspace."

James encouraged the team to declutter their workstations, disposing of items that were no longer needed and organizing remaining items for easy access.

Implementing 5S: Set in Order

Next, the team moved on to the second step of 5S: Set in Order. They organized their work areas, arranging tools, materials, and equipment in a logical and efficient manner.

Sarah demonstrated, "Setting in order ensures that everything has a designated place and is easily accessible when needed. This reduces wasted time searching for items and minimizes the risk of errors."

James guided the team as they labeled storage bins, marked floor boundaries, and created visual cues to indicate proper tool placement and workflow.

Implementing 5S: Shine

With their work areas organized, the team proceeded to the third step of 5S: Shine. They cleaned and sanitized their workstations, machinery, and equipment to ensure optimal performance and safety.

Sarah emphasized, "Shining not only improves the appearance of our work environment but also helps identify and eliminate sources of contamination, defects, and inefficiencies."

James distributed cleaning supplies and encouraged the team to thoroughly clean their work areas, paying attention to hidden corners, equipment surfaces, and tool storage areas.

Implementing 5S: Standardize

Once their work areas were clean and organized, the team focused on the fourth step of 5S: Standardize. They developed standardized procedures and protocols to maintain the improvements made during the previous steps.

Sarah reminded the team, "Standardizing ensures that everyone follows the same procedures and maintains the cleanliness and organization of their work areas consistently."

James led the team in documenting standardized procedures for cleaning, organizing, and maintaining their work areas, creating visual checklists and guidelines for reference.

Implementing 5S: Sustain

Finally, the team addressed the fifth step of 5S: Sustain. They committed to sustaining the improvements made through regular audits, training, and continuous reinforcement of 5S principles.

Sarah encouraged the team, "Sustaining our improvements requires ongoing commitment and discipline. By making 5S a part of our daily routine, we can ensure that our work environment remains clean, organized, and efficient."

James scheduled regular 5S audits and training sessions to reinforce the importance of maintaining the improvements made and to address any issues or challenges that arose.

Conducting Kaizen Events

After completing the 5S implementation, the team embarked on Kaizen events to tackle specific process improvements. They formed cross-functional teams, identified areas for improvement, and developed action plans to drive positive change.

Sarah explained, "Kaizen events allow us to make rapid improvements to our processes by bringing together diverse perspectives and expertise. By working collaboratively, we can identify waste, streamline workflows, and drive efficiency gains."

James facilitated the Kaizen events, guiding the teams through problem-solving exercises, brainstorming sessions, and root cause analysis to identify and prioritize improvement opportunities.

Applying Poka-Yoke Principles

Finally, the team applied Poka-Yoke principles to their processes to prevent errors and defects. They implemented error-proofing devices, visual cues, and process controls to ensure that mistakes were detected and corrected before they could impact quality or performance.

Sarah demonstrated, "Poka-Yoke helps us design our processes in a way that makes errors impossible or easily detectable. By incorporating foolproofing mechanisms and mistake-proofing devices, we can minimize the risk of defects and ensure consistent quality."

James guided the team as they installed sensors, alarms, and warning signs to alert operators of potential errors or deviations from standard procedures.

Conclusion: Driving Continuous Improvement

As the day drew to a close, Sarah and James gathered the team for a debriefing session. They reflected on the progress made and the impact of implementing Lean tools on their processes.

Sarah concluded, "Today, we've made significant strides toward eliminating waste and driving continuous improvement in our processes. By embracing 5S, conducting Kaizen events, and applying Poka-Yoke principles, we've created a workplace that is organized, efficient, and error-free."

James nodded in agreement, "Let's continue to leverage these Lean tools and principles as we strive for operational excellence and deliver greater value to our customers and our business."

The team left the factory floor feeling empowered and inspired, ready to apply their newfound knowledge and skills to drive positive change in their processes. With Lean tools at their disposal, Aurora Electronics was well-equipped to achieve their goals of waste elimination and continuous improvement.

Case Studies: Waste Elimination Successes

The Aurora Electronics leadership team gathered in the boardroom for a special presentation on waste elimination successes. Sarah Mitchell and James Thompson stood at the front, ready to share real-world examples of how waste elimination strategies had driven positive change in various organizations.

Sarah began, "Good afternoon, everyone. Today, we'll be discussing case studies of companies that have successfully eliminated waste from their processes. These case studies will provide valuable insights and inspiration as we continue our own journey of waste elimination and process improvement."

James added, "By studying these success stories, we can learn from the experiences of others and apply their strategies and techniques to our own operations."

Case Study 1: Toyota's Lean Transformation

Sarah started with the iconic example of Toyota's Lean transformation. "Toyota is renowned for its commitment to waste elimination through its Toyota Production System.

By implementing Lean principles such as Just-in-Time production and Kanban systems, Toyota has significantly reduced waste, improved efficiency, and maintained high levels of quality."

James elaborated, "Toyota's focus on continuous improvement and respect for people has enabled them to create a culture of waste elimination, where every employee is empowered to identify and eliminate waste in their processes."

Case Study 2: Boeing's Lean Manufacturing

The next slide displayed Boeing's logo. "Boeing implemented Lean principles to streamline its manufacturing processes and reduce waste in aircraft production," Sarah explained.

James continued, "By optimizing workflows, reducing lead times, and implementing Lean tools such as Value Stream Mapping and Kaizen events, Boeing achieved significant cost savings, improved quality, and increased productivity."

Case Study 3: Starbucks' 5S Success

Sarah switched to Starbucks' logo. "Starbucks applied the principles of 5S to its store operations, resulting in cleaner, more organized workspaces and improved efficiency," she said.

James shared, "Through the implementation of Sort, Set in Order, Shine, Standardize, and Sustain, Starbucks reduced clutter, improved employee morale, and enhanced the overall customer experience."

Case Study 4: Amazon's Poka-Yoke Implementation

The next slide featured Amazon's logo. "Amazon utilized Poka-Yoke principles to prevent errors and defects in its fulfillment centers," Sarah explained.

James highlighted, "By implementing error-proofing devices, such as barcode scanners and automated quality checks, Amazon minimized the risk of picking errors, reduced returns, and improved customer satisfaction."

Case Study 5: Ford's Kaizen Success

The final slide displayed Ford's logo. "Ford Motor Company implemented Kaizen events to drive continuous improvement in its manufacturing processes," Sarah said.

James concluded, "Through cross-functional collaboration and rapid problem-solving, Ford identified and eliminated waste, reduced production lead times, and improved product quality, positioning itself as a leader in the automotive industry."

Discussion and Application

Sarah opened the floor for discussion. "These case studies demonstrate the power of waste elimination strategies in driving positive change and achieving operational excellence. Let's discuss how we can apply these lessons to our own operations at Aurora Electronics."

The team engaged in a lively discussion, drawing parallels between the case studies and their own challenges and opportunities. They brainstormed ideas for implementing Lean principles, conducting Kaizen events, and applying Poka-Yoke techniques to their processes.

Conclusion: Driving Success Through Waste Elimination

James wrapped up the presentation with a note of encouragement. "By learning from these successful case studies and applying the principles of waste elimination to our own operations, we can drive positive change, improve efficiency, and achieve our goals of operational excellence."

Sarah nodded in agreement. "Let's use these insights to guide our waste elimination efforts and ensure that every action we take adds value to our customers and contributes to the success of Aurora Electronics."

The team left the boardroom inspired and motivated, armed with valuable insights from the waste elimination case studies. With a clear understanding of the strategies and techniques that had driven success in other organizations, Aurora Electronics was well-equipped to achieve their goals of waste elimination and process improvement.

Sustaining Waste Reduction Efforts

The Aurora Electronics continuous improvement team gathered in the conference room for a discussion on sustaining waste reduction efforts. Sarah Mitchell and James Thompson led the meeting, ready to explore strategies for maintaining the gains achieved through waste elimination.

Sarah began, "Good morning, everyone. Today, we're going to focus on sustaining our waste reduction efforts. It's not enough to eliminate waste once; we must ensure that our improvements are maintained over the long term. By embedding waste reduction principles into our culture and processes, we can create a sustainable foundation for continuous improvement."

James added, "Let's brainstorm ideas and develop a plan for sustaining our waste reduction efforts effectively."

Embedding Waste Reduction into Company Culture

Sarah emphasized the importance of fostering a culture of waste reduction throughout the organization. "To sustain our waste reduction efforts, we must ensure that waste elimination becomes a core value embraced by every member of our team."

James suggested, "We can achieve this by promoting awareness and education about waste reduction principles, recognizing and rewarding employees for their contributions to waste elimination, and integrating waste reduction goals into performance evaluations and KPIs."

Continuous Training and Development

Sarah proposed implementing ongoing training and development programs to keep employees engaged and informed about waste reduction strategies. "By providing regular training sessions, workshops, and refresher courses, we can ensure that everyone understands their role in waste elimination and remains committed to continuous improvement."

James agreed, "Training should cover not only the principles of waste reduction but also practical techniques and tools for identifying and eliminating waste in specific processes. By empowering our team with the knowledge and skills they need, we can sustain our waste reduction efforts effectively."

Regular Monitoring and Auditing

Sarah highlighted the importance of regular monitoring and auditing to track progress and identify areas for improvement. "By conducting regular audits and performance reviews, we can ensure that our waste reduction efforts are on track and that any deviations are addressed promptly."

James suggested, "Audits should focus on key metrics such as inventory levels, process cycle times, defect rates, and workplace organization. By monitoring these metrics closely, we can identify trends, root causes, and opportunities for further waste reduction."

Employee Engagement and Empowerment

Sarah encouraged fostering employee engagement and empowerment to sustain waste reduction efforts. "By involving employees in problem-solving, decision-making, and process improvement initiatives, we can tap into their creativity, expertise, and commitment to drive continuous improvement."

James proposed, "We can establish cross-functional teams, task forces, or suggestion programs to encourage employees to share their ideas and contribute to waste elimination efforts. By empowering employees to take ownership of waste reduction, we can create a culture of continuous improvement that sustains over time."

Celebrating Successes and Sharing Best Practices

Sarah concluded the meeting by emphasizing the importance of celebrating successes and sharing best practices to sustain waste reduction efforts. "By recognizing and celebrating achievements, we can reinforce the importance of waste reduction and inspire others to follow suit."

James suggested, "We can create forums, newsletters, or online platforms to share success stories, case studies, and lessons learned from waste reduction initiatives. By highlighting best practices and success stories, we can inspire and motivate others to replicate similar achievements in their own areas."

Conclusion: Commitment to Continuous Improvement

As the meeting drew to a close, Sarah and James thanked the team for their participation and commitment to sustaining waste reduction efforts. "By working together and embedding waste reduction principles into our culture and processes, we can create a sustainable foundation for continuous improvement and achieve our goals of operational excellence."

The team left the meeting with a renewed sense of purpose and commitment to sustaining waste reduction efforts. With a clear plan in place and the support of the entire organization, Aurora Electronics was well-positioned to maintain their gains and drive continuous improvement for years to come.

5

Chapter 5: Continuous Improvement (Kaizen)

The Philosophy of Kaizen

The auditorium at Aurora Electronics buzzed with anticipation as employees gathered for a seminar on the philosophy of Kaizen. Sarah Mitchell and James Thompson stood at the front of the room, ready to delve into the principles that underpin continuous improvement.

Sarah began, "Good morning, everyone. Today, we're going to explore the philosophy of Kaizen, a cornerstone of Lean management. Kaizen, which translates to 'change for the better' in Japanese, emphasizes continuous improvement in all aspects of our work and lives."

James added, "Kaizen is not just a set of tools or techniques; it's a mindset, a way of thinking that drives us to constantly seek out opportunities for improvement, no matter how small."

The Spirit of Kaizen

Sarah continued, "At its core, Kaizen is about making incremental improvements every day, in every process, and in every interaction. It's about fostering a culture of continuous learning, adaptation, and innovation."

James elaborated, "Kaizen encourages us to challenge the status quo, to question our assumptions, and to strive for excellence in everything we do. It's about embracing change as a catalyst for growth and progress."

The Three Pillars of Kaizen

Sarah introduced the three pillars of Kaizen: Standardization, Elimination of Waste, and Empowerment of Employees. "These pillars provide a framework for continuous improvement and guide our actions as we strive to achieve our goals."

James explained, "Standardization ensures consistency and stability in our processes, making it easier to identify and address areas for improvement. Elimination of Waste focuses on streamlining processes and reducing inefficiencies to deliver greater value to our customers. Empowerment of Employees involves engaging and empowering our team members to contribute their ideas and expertise to the improvement process."

Kaizen in Practice: A Case Study

Sarah shared a case study of a company that embraced the philosophy of Kaizen to transform its operations and achieve remarkable results. "By implementing Kaizen principles such as Gemba Walks, 5S, and continuous training and development, this company was able to reduce lead times, improve quality, and increase customer satisfaction."

James highlighted, "Through the relentless pursuit of improvement and a commitment to excellence, this company not only survived but thrived in a competitive marketplace.

Their success serves as a testament to the power of Kaizen to drive positive change and achieve sustainable growth."

Conclusion: Embracing the Kaizen Mindset

As the seminar concluded, Sarah and James encouraged the audience to embrace the Kaizen mindset in their work and lives. "By adopting the philosophy of Kaizen and making continuous improvement a part of our daily routine, we can unlock our full potential and achieve our goals of excellence and success."

James nodded in agreement, "Let's challenge ourselves to embrace change, to seek out opportunities for improvement, and to strive for excellence in everything we do. Together, we can create a culture of continuous improvement that drives us toward our shared vision of a better future."

The audience left the auditorium inspired and energized, ready to apply the principles of Kaizen to their work and lives. With a newfound appreciation for the philosophy of continuous improvement, Aurora Electronics was well-equipped to embark on their journey toward excellence and success.

Implementing Kaizen in the Workplace

The conference room at Aurora Electronics buzzed with anticipation as employees gathered for a workshop on implementing Kaizen in the workplace. Sarah Mitchell and James Thompson stood at the front of the room, ready to guide the team through the process of applying Kaizen principles to their daily work.

Sarah began, "Good morning, everyone. Today, we're going to explore how we can implement Kaizen in our workplace to drive continuous improvement and achieve our goals of operational excellence."

James added, "Kaizen is about making small, incremental improvements every day. It's not about radical changes or grand gestures; it's about identifying opportunities for improvement and taking action to address them."

Identifying Improvement Opportunities

Sarah encouraged the team to start by identifying improvement opportunities in their processes and workflows. "Kaizen begins with observation and reflection. Take a step back and examine your work environment with a critical eye. Look for inefficiencies, bottlenecks, and areas where things could be done better."

James provided guidance, "Ask yourselves questions like: What wastes do you see? Where are the pain points in your processes? What opportunities for improvement do you notice?"

Kaizen Events and Rapid Improvement Workshops

Sarah introduced Kaizen events and rapid improvement workshops as effective tools for driving continuous improvement. "Kaizen events are focused, short-term improvement projects aimed at addressing specific problems or opportunities for improvement. They bring together cross-functional teams to brainstorm ideas, implement solutions, and monitor results."

James elaborated, "During a Kaizen event, participants work together to identify root causes, develop action plans, and implement changes rapidly. By focusing on a single issue or process, we can achieve significant improvements in a short amount of time."

Gemba Walks and Daily Kaizen

Sarah emphasized the importance of Gemba Walks and daily Kaizen activities in fostering a culture of continuous improvement. "Gemba Walks involve going to the 'gemba,' or the place where the work is done, to observe processes firsthand, identify waste, and engage with frontline employees."

James encouraged the team, "Make Gemba Walks a regular practice in your work routine. Engage with your colleagues, ask questions, and listen to their ideas for improvement. By involving everyone in the improvement process, we can tap into the collective wisdom of our team and drive positive change."

PDCA Cycle: Plan, Do, Check, Act

Sarah introduced the PDCA (Plan, Do, Check, Act) cycle as a framework for continuous improvement. "The PDCA cycle provides a systematic approach to problem-solving and improvement. It begins with planning and goal setting, followed by implementation, evaluation, and adjustment."

James explained, "By following the PDCA cycle, we can test our ideas, measure their impact, and make adjustments as needed to achieve our desired outcomes. It's a dynamic and iterative process that allows us to continuously learn and improve."

Conclusion: Empowering Continuous Improvement

As the workshop concluded, Sarah and James reminded the team that implementing Kaizen is a journey, not a destination. "By embracing the principles of Kaizen and making continuous improvement a part of our daily work, we can unlock our full potential and achieve our goals of excellence and success."

James nodded in agreement, "Let's commit ourselves to the Kaizen mindset, to seeking out opportunities for improvement, and to taking action to address them. Together, we can create a workplace that is constantly evolving, innovating, and improving."

The team left the workshop feeling inspired and empowered, ready to apply the principles of Kaizen to their work and lives. With a clear roadmap for implementing Kaizen in the workplace, Aurora Electronics was well-equipped to drive continuous improvement and achieve their goals of operational excellence.

Kaizen Events and Workshops

Excitement filled the air on the factory floor of Aurora Electronics as teams gathered for a Kaizen event kickoff. Sarah Mitchell and James Thompson stood at the front, ready to guide the teams through a focused improvement project aimed at driving positive change.

Sarah began, "Good morning, everyone. Today marks the beginning of our Kaizen event, a dedicated effort to identify and implement improvements in our processes. By working together as a team, we can achieve significant gains in efficiency, quality, and customer satisfaction."

James added, "During this Kaizen event, we'll be focusing on a specific area or process, brainstorming ideas for improvement, and implementing changes rapidly. Let's dive in and make a difference!"

Defining the Scope and Goals

Sarah kicked off the event by defining the scope and goals of the Kaizen project. "Our goal for this Kaizen event is to reduce setup times in our production line by 50% within the next week. By streamlining our setup processes, we can increase productivity, reduce lead times, and better meet customer demand."

James outlined the objectives, "We'll start by mapping out our current setup process, identifying inefficiencies and opportunities for improvement. Then, we'll brainstorm ideas for reducing setup times and prioritize our actions based on impact and feasibility."

Gemba Walk and Process Observation

Sarah led the team on a Gemba Walk to observe the setup process firsthand. "Let's go to the gemba, the place where the work is done, to observe the setup process and identify opportunities for improvement."

James encouraged active participation, "As we observe the setup process, pay attention to any bottlenecks, delays, or unnecessary steps. Think about how we can streamline the process to make it more efficient and effective."

Brainstorming Ideas for Improvement

Back in the conference room, teams gathered to brainstorm ideas for improvement. Sarah facilitated the discussion, "Let's generate as many ideas as possible for reducing setup times. No idea is too small or too ambitious. Think creatively and outside the box."

James encouraged collaboration, "Build on each other's ideas and explore innovative solutions. Remember, the goal is to find ways to make our setup process faster, smoother, and more efficient."

Developing Action Plans

Once ideas were generated, teams worked to develop action plans for implementing their proposed improvements. Sarah guided the teams through the process, "Let's break down our ideas into actionable steps, assign responsibilities, and establish timelines for implementation."

James provided support, "Consider potential obstacles and develop contingency plans to address them. By thinking ahead and planning carefully, we can ensure the success of our improvement initiatives."

Implementation and Rapid Improvement

With action plans in place, teams wasted no time in implementing their proposed improvements. Sarah and James provided support and guidance as teams worked to implement changes rapidly.

Sarah cheered on the teams, "Keep up the momentum and focus on driving positive change. Every small improvement we make brings us closer to our goal of reducing setup times and improving our overall efficiency."

Monitoring and Evaluation

Throughout the Kaizen event, Sarah and James monitored progress and evaluated the impact of the implemented improvements. They conducted regular check-ins with teams to assess results, address challenges, and provide support as needed.

Sarah encouraged perseverance, "Stay committed to our goals and keep pushing forward. By monitoring our progress and making adjustments as needed, we can ensure that we achieve our objectives and deliver tangible results."

Celebrating Successes and Lessons Learned

As the Kaizen event came to a close, Sarah and James gathered the teams to celebrate their successes and reflect on lessons learned. They recognized the hard work and dedication of team members and highlighted the positive impact of the implemented improvements.

James expressed gratitude, "Thank you to everyone for your contributions to this Kaizen event. Your creativity, teamwork, and commitment to continuous improvement have been truly inspiring."

Conclusion: Driving Continuous Improvement

As the teams dispersed, Sarah and James reflected on the success of the Kaizen event. "By embracing Kaizen principles and working together as a team, we've achieved significant improvements in our setup process. Let's carry this momentum forward and continue to drive continuous improvement in all aspects of our work."

James nodded in agreement, "With the Kaizen mindset guiding us, there's no limit to what we can achieve. Let's keep pushing the boundaries, challenging the status quo, and striving for excellence in everything we do."

The factory floor buzzed with energy and excitement as teams returned to their workstations, inspired to apply the lessons learned from the Kaizen event to drive further improvements. With a renewed sense of purpose and commitment to continuous improvement, Aurora Electronics was well-equipped to achieve their goals of operational excellence and customer satisfaction.

Measuring Kaizen Success

In the boardroom of Aurora Electronics, the leadership team gathered for a review of the success metrics from recent Kaizen events. Sarah Mitchell and James Thompson led the discussion, ready to assess the impact of the implemented improvements on key performance indicators.

Sarah began, "Good morning, everyone. Today, we'll be reviewing the success metrics from our recent Kaizen events to assess the impact of the implemented improvements on our processes and performance."

James added, "By measuring the success of our Kaizen initiatives, we can evaluate our progress, identify areas for further improvement, and celebrate our achievements."

Defining Key Performance Indicators (KPIs)

Sarah kicked off the meeting by defining the key performance indicators (KPIs) that would be used to measure the success of the Kaizen initiatives. "Our KPIs include metrics such as setup times, defect rates, productivity levels, and customer satisfaction scores."

James elaborated, "These KPIs provide a comprehensive view of the impact of the implemented improvements on our processes, quality, and customer experience. By tracking these metrics over time, we can gauge the effectiveness of our Kaizen initiatives and identify opportunities for further optimization."

Analyzing Performance Data

The team delved into the performance data from recent Kaizen events, analyzing trends, patterns, and outliers. Sarah guided the discussion, "Let's review the data and identify any improvements or areas for concern. Are there any noticeable trends or patterns that we should be aware of?"

James facilitated the analysis, "Look for any significant changes in our KPIs following the implementation of Kaizen improvements. Are setup times decreasing? Are defect rates declining? Are productivity levels improving? Let's dig deep and uncover the impact of our efforts."

Celebrating Successes

As the team reviewed the performance data, they celebrated successes and achievements resulting from the implemented Kaizen improvements. Sarah commended the team, "Congratulations to everyone on the positive outcomes of our Kaizen initiatives. Your hard work, creativity, and dedication have made a tangible difference in our processes and performance."

James echoed the sentiment, "Let's take a moment to recognize the teams involved in the Kaizen events and applaud their contributions to our success. Your commitment to continuous improvement is truly inspiring."

Identifying Areas for Further Improvement

While celebrating successes, the team also identified areas for further improvement and optimization. Sarah encouraged a proactive approach, "As we review the data, let's not overlook opportunities for further optimization. Are there any areas where performance could be enhanced? Are there any new challenges or emerging trends that we need to address?"

James facilitated a discussion on potential areas for improvement, "Let's brainstorm ideas for addressing any gaps or weaknesses identified in the data. By leveraging the insights gained from our analysis, we can develop action plans to drive further improvements and ensure sustained success."

Commitment to Continuous Improvement

As the meeting concluded, Sarah and James reaffirmed the team's commitment to continuous improvement. "By measuring the success of our Kaizen initiatives, we can identify opportunities for further optimization and drive ongoing improvement in our processes and performance."

James nodded in agreement, "Let's continue to embrace the Kaizen mindset, to seek out opportunities for improvement, and to take action to address them. Together, we can achieve our goals of excellence and success."

The team left the boardroom feeling inspired and motivated, ready to apply the insights gained from the success metrics review to drive further improvements in their processes and performance. With a clear focus on continuous improvement, Aurora Electronics was well-positioned to achieve their goals of operational excellence and customer satisfaction.

Case Studies: Kaizen in Action

In the conference room at Aurora Electronics, employees gathered for a presentation on case studies showcasing Kaizen in action. Sarah Mitchell and James Thompson stood at the front of the room, ready to share real-world examples of how Kaizen principles had driven positive change in various processes and organizations.

Sarah began, "Good afternoon, everyone. Today, we're going to explore case studies that highlight the power of Kaizen to drive continuous improvement and achieve remarkable results."

James added, "These case studies demonstrate how Kaizen principles such as Gemba Walks, 5S, and the PDCA cycle have been applied in different contexts to overcome challenges, optimize processes, and deliver value to customers."

Case Study 1: Reducing Setup Times

Sarah introduced the first case study, "Our first case study focuses on a manufacturing company that sought to reduce setup times on its production line. By implementing Kaizen principles such as standardized work, visual management, and cross-functional teamwork, the company was able to achieve a 30% reduction in setup times within three months."

James elaborated, "Through the use of SMED (Single-Minute Exchange of Die) techniques and regular Gemba Walks, the company identified and eliminated waste in its setup processes, resulting in improved efficiency, reduced lead times, and increased customer satisfaction."

Case Study 2: Improving Order Fulfillment

The next slide displayed a case study of a distribution center that implemented Kaizen principles to improve order fulfillment processes. "Facing increasing customer demand and tight deadlines, the distribution center embarked on a Kaizen journey to streamline its order fulfillment processes," Sarah explained.

James shared, "By mapping out value streams, implementing visual management tools such as Kanban boards, and empowering frontline employees to suggest and implement improvements, the distribution center achieved a 25% reduction in order processing times and a 20% increase in order accuracy."

Case Study 3: Enhancing Office Efficiency

The presentation shifted to a case study of an office environment where Kaizen principles were applied to enhance efficiency and productivity. "In this case study, a corporate office implemented Kaizen initiatives to streamline administrative processes and improve workflow," Sarah said.

James highlighted, "By implementing 5S methodology to organize workspaces, standardizing procedures through the use of standardized work instructions, and fostering a culture of continuous improvement through regular Kaizen events, the office achieved a 15% increase in productivity and a 20% reduction in error rates."

Case Study 4: Boosting Customer Satisfaction

The final case study showcased a service-oriented company that leveraged Kaizen principles to boost customer satisfaction. "In this case study, a service-oriented company implemented Kaizen initiatives to improve customer service processes and enhance the overall customer experience," Sarah explained.

James shared, "By implementing customer feedback loops, conducting Gemba Walks to better understand customer needs, and empowering frontline employees to make real-time improvements to service delivery, the company achieved a 30% increase in customer satisfaction scores and a 25% decrease in customer complaints."

Conclusion: Inspiring Kaizen Success Stories

As the presentation concluded, Sarah and James expressed their gratitude to the audience for their engagement and participation. "These case studies serve as inspiring examples of the transformative power of Kaizen to drive continuous improvement and achieve remarkable results," Sarah said.

James nodded in agreement, "Let's draw inspiration from these success stories and apply the principles of Kaizen to our own work and lives. By embracing the Kaizen mindset and making continuous improvement a part of our daily routine, we can unlock our full potential and achieve our goals of excellence and success."

The audience left the conference room feeling inspired and motivated, ready to apply the insights gained from the Kaizen case studies to drive continuous improvement in their own processes and organizations. With a clear understanding of the impact of Kaizen in action, Aurora Electronics was well-equipped to achieve their goals of operational excellence and customer satisfaction.

Overcoming Resistance to Continuous Improvement

In the staff meeting at Aurora Electronics, Sarah Mitchell and James Thompson addressed the topic of overcoming resistance to continuous improvement. Aware that change often met resistance, they aimed to equip their team with strategies to embrace and drive forward continuous improvement efforts.

Sarah began, "Good morning, everyone. Today, we're going to discuss overcoming resistance to continuous improvement and how we can effectively navigate challenges on our journey towards operational excellence."

James added, "As we embark on our continuous improvement initiatives, it's natural to encounter resistance to change. However, by understanding the root causes of resistance and implementing strategies to address them, we can foster a culture of openness, collaboration, and innovation."

Understanding the Sources of Resistance

Sarah encouraged the team to understand the sources of resistance to change. "Resistance to continuous improvement can stem from various factors, including fear of the unknown, perceived loss of control, and resistance to change itself."

James elaborated, "It's important to acknowledge that change can be unsettling and disruptive. By understanding the reasons behind resistance, we can address concerns, alleviate fears, and engage our team in the change process."

Communicating the Vision and Benefits

Sarah emphasized the importance of clear communication in overcoming resistance to continuous improvement. "Communicating the vision, goals, and benefits of continuous improvement initiatives can help align our team and inspire commitment to change."

James nodded in agreement, "Be transparent about the reasons for change and the expected outcomes. Highlight the positive impact of continuous improvement on our processes, performance, and overall success."

Engaging Stakeholders and Soliciting Feedback

Sarah encouraged engaging stakeholders and soliciting feedback to overcome resistance to continuous improvement. "Involve key stakeholders in the change process, seek their input and perspective, and address their concerns and objections."

James added, "By actively involving stakeholders in the decision-making process, we can build buy-in, ownership, and commitment to change. Create opportunities for open dialogue, feedback, and collaboration to ensure that everyone feels heard and valued."

Empowering Employees and Celebrating Successes

Sarah highlighted the importance of empowering employees and celebrating successes in overcoming resistance to continuous improvement. "Empower employees to take ownership of change, contribute their ideas and expertise, and play an active role in driving continuous improvement."

James nodded, "Celebrate successes and milestones along the way to recognize the contributions of our team and reinforce the benefits of continuous improvement. By acknowledging progress and achievements, we can inspire motivation and momentum for further change."

Leading by Example and Fostering a Culture of Innovation

Sarah concluded the discussion by emphasizing the role

of leadership in overcoming resistance to continuous improvement. "Lead by example, demonstrate a commitment to continuous improvement, and champion change initiatives throughout the organization."

James nodded, "Foster a culture of innovation, experimentation, and learning where taking risks and embracing change are encouraged and rewarded. By creating an environment where continuous improvement is valued and celebrated, we can overcome resistance and drive positive change."

Conclusion: Embracing Continuous Improvement

As the meeting concluded, Sarah and James thanked the team for their participation and commitment to continuous improvement. "By understanding the sources of resistance, communicating the vision and benefits, engaging stakeholders, empowering employees, leading by example, and fostering a culture of innovation, we can overcome resistance to change and drive continuous improvement in our processes and performance."

James nodded in agreement, "Let's embrace the challenges and opportunities of continuous improvement, support each other on our journey, and strive for excellence in everything we do. Together, we can achieve our goals of operational excellence and customer satisfaction."

The team left the meeting feeling empowered and inspired, ready to embrace continuous improvement and drive positive change in their processes and organization. With a clear understanding of how to overcome resistance to change, Aurora Electronics was well-equipped to achieve their goals and aspirations.

6

Chapter 6: Just-In-Time (JIT) Production

Principles of JIT

On the bustling factory floor of Aurora Electronics, employees gathered for a training session on the principles of Just-In-Time (JIT) production. Sarah Mitchell and James Thompson stood at the front of the room, ready to introduce the team to the fundamental concepts of JIT.

Sarah began, "Good morning, everyone. Today, we're going to explore the principles of Just-In-Time (JIT) production, a cornerstone of Lean manufacturing. JIT is all about delivering the right quantity of products at the right time, in the right place, and with the right quality."

James added, "By embracing JIT principles, we can eliminate waste, reduce lead times, improve efficiency, and enhance customer satisfaction. Let's dive in and explore the key principles of JIT."

Principle 1: Elimination of Waste

Sarah explained the first principle of JIT, "At the heart of JIT is the elimination of waste. Waste in the form of overproduction, excess inventory, unnecessary transportation, and waiting times can lead to inefficiencies and added costs."

James elaborated, "By implementing JIT, we aim to produce only what is needed, when it is needed, and in the exact quantity required. This allows us to minimize inventory, reduce storage space, and avoid the costs associated with excess production."

Principle 2: Pull System

Sarah introduced the concept of the pull system, "In a JIT environment, production is driven by customer demand rather than forecasted projections. This means that we only produce items when they are requested by the customer, creating a 'pull' rather than a 'push' system."

James emphasized, "By implementing a pull system, we can better align production with actual demand, reduce the risk of overproduction, and minimize the buildup of excess inventory. This enables us to respond quickly to changes in customer demand and deliver products with greater agility."

Principle 3: Continuous Improvement

Sarah highlighted the importance of continuous improvement in JIT production, "JIT is not a one-time implementation but a continuous journey of improvement. By continuously seeking out opportunities to streamline processes, reduce lead times, and enhance efficiency, we can achieve ongoing improvements in our operations."

James nodded, "Through the relentless pursuit of perfection and the commitment to continuous improvement, we can drive waste out of our processes, optimize production flows, and deliver greater value to our customers."

Principle 4: Flexibility and Adaptability

Sarah discussed the principles of flexibility and adaptability in JIT production, "In a JIT environment, it's essential to be flexible and adaptable to changes in customer demand, market conditions, and production requirements. This requires the ability to quickly adjust production schedules, changeover times, and resource allocations."

James emphasized, "By building flexibility and adaptability into our processes, we can respond rapidly to fluctuations in demand, minimize lead times, and maximize efficiency. This enables us to meet customer needs more effectively and maintain a competitive edge in the marketplace."

Conclusion: Embracing JIT Principles

As the training session concluded, Sarah and James encouraged the team to embrace the principles of JIT in their work and lives. "By eliminating waste, implementing pull systems, fostering a culture of continuous improvement, and embracing flexibility and adaptability, we can unlock the full potential of JIT production and achieve our goals of operational excellence and customer satisfaction."

James nodded in agreement, "Let's commit ourselves to the JIT mindset, to delivering products with precision, efficiency, and quality. Together, we can optimize our processes, reduce waste, and create value for our customers."

The team left the training session feeling inspired and motivated, ready to apply the principles of JIT production to their work on the factory floor. With a clear understanding of the fundamental concepts of JIT, Aurora Electronics was well-equipped to embark on their journey towards JIT excellence.

Benefits of JIT Production

In the management meeting at Aurora Electronics, Sarah Mitchell and James Thompson led a discussion on the benefits of Just-In-Time (JIT) production. Gathered around the conference table, the leadership team eagerly delved into the advantages of implementing JIT principles in their manufacturing processes.

Sarah began, "Good afternoon, everyone. Today, we're going to explore the benefits of Just-In-Time (JIT) production and how it can transform our operations and enhance our competitiveness in the marketplace."

James added, "By embracing JIT principles such as waste elimination, pull systems, continuous improvement, and flexibility, we can achieve significant improvements in efficiency, quality, and customer satisfaction. Let's dive in and explore the benefits of JIT production."

Benefit 1: Reduced Inventory Costs

Sarah highlighted the first benefit of JIT production, "One of the primary advantages of JIT is the reduction in inventory costs. By producing only what is needed, when it is needed, and in the exact quantity required, we can minimize inventory levels and free up valuable capital that would otherwise be tied up in excess inventory."

James elaborated, "Reducing inventory costs allows us to optimize cash flow, minimize storage space, and avoid the risks associated with holding excess inventory, such as obsolescence and deterioration. This enables us to operate more efficiently and invest resources in other areas of our business."

Benefit 2: Increased Efficiency

Sarah discussed the second benefit of JIT production, "JIT enables us to achieve higher levels of efficiency by eliminating waste, streamlining processes, and optimizing production flows. By focusing on value-added activities and reducing non-value-added activities, we can improve productivity and throughput."

James nodded, "Increased efficiency allows us to produce more with less, reducing lead times, improving on-time delivery performance, and enhancing overall operational performance. This enables us to meet customer demand more effectively and respond quickly to changes in market conditions."

Benefit 3: Enhanced Quality

Sarah emphasized the third benefit of JIT production, "JIT places a strong emphasis on quality throughout the production process. By eliminating waste and continuously improving processes, we can reduce defects, errors, and rework, leading to higher levels of product quality and customer satisfaction."

James added, "Enhanced quality not only improves customer satisfaction but also reduces costs associated with scrap, rework, and warranty claims. By delivering products of consistently high quality, we can build trust and loyalty with our customers and strengthen our competitive position in the marketplace."

Benefit 4: Improved Customer Responsiveness

Sarah discussed the fourth benefit of JIT production, "JIT enables us to be more responsive to customer demand by producing goods in direct response to customer orders. By implementing pull systems and minimizing lead times, we can reduce the time it takes to fulfill customer orders and improve our overall responsiveness."

James nodded, "Improved customer responsiveness allows us to better meet customer needs, reduce order cycle times, and enhance the overall customer experience. This enables us to build strong relationships with our customers and differentiate ourselves from competitors in the marketplace."

Conclusion: Realizing the Benefits of JIT Production

As the meeting concluded, Sarah and James reiterated the importance of embracing JIT production to realize its many benefits. "By reducing inventory costs, increasing efficiency, enhancing quality, and improving customer responsiveness, we can achieve significant improvements in our operations and deliver greater value to our customers," Sarah said.

James nodded in agreement, "Let's commit ourselves to the JIT mindset, to delivering products with precision, efficiency, and quality. Together, we can optimize our processes, reduce waste, and create value for our customers."

The leadership team left the meeting feeling energized and motivated, ready to leverage the benefits of JIT production to drive success and competitiveness in their manufacturing operations. With a clear understanding of the advantages of JIT, Aurora Electronics was well-positioned to achieve their goals of operational excellence and customer satisfaction.

Implementing JIT in Your Organization

In a strategy session at Aurora Electronics, Sarah Mitchell and James Thompson led a discussion on the implementation of Just-In-Time (JIT) production in the organization. Surrounded by whiteboards filled with diagrams and charts, the team eagerly brainstormed strategies to embrace JIT principles and transform their manufacturing processes.

Sarah began, "Good morning, everyone. Today, we're going to discuss how we can implement Just-In-Time (JIT) production in our organization to achieve greater efficiency, quality, and customer satisfaction."

James added, "By adopting JIT principles such as waste elimination, pull systems, continuous improvement, and flexibility, we can optimize our processes and deliver products with precision and agility. Let's explore strategies for implementing JIT in our organization."

Step 1: Assess Current Processes and Identify Opportunities for Improvement

Sarah highlighted the first step in implementing JIT, "Before we can embrace JIT principles, we need to assess our current processes and identify opportunities for improvement. This involves mapping out our value streams, analyzing production flows, and identifying areas of waste and inefficiency."

James nodded, "By conducting Gemba Walks, engaging frontline employees, and soliciting feedback from stakeholders, we can gain valuable insights into our operations and uncover opportunities for optimization."

Step 2: Establish Pull Systems and Kanban Systems

Sarah discussed the next step in implementing JIT, "Once we've identified opportunities for improvement, we can begin to establish pull systems and Kanban systems to drive production based on customer demand."

James elaborated, "By implementing pull systems, we can minimize inventory levels, reduce lead times, and respond quickly to changes in customer demand. Kanban systems provide visual signals that trigger production and replenishment activities, ensuring that we produce only what is needed, when it is needed."

Step 3: Streamline Production Processes and Eliminate Waste

Sarah emphasized the importance of streamlining production processes and eliminating waste, "As we implement JIT, we must focus on streamlining our production processes and eliminating waste in all its forms. This involves standardizing work procedures, reducing setup times, and optimizing workflow."

James added, "By implementing tools and techniques such as 5S, SMED, and Total Productive Maintenance (TPM), we can create a culture of continuous improvement and drive waste out of our processes. This enables us to achieve higher levels of efficiency and quality in our operations."

Step 4: Foster a Culture of Continuous Improvement

Sarah discussed the importance of fostering a culture of continuous improvement, "JIT is not a one-time implementation but a continuous journey of improvement. It's essential to engage employees, empower teams, and foster a culture of innovation and collaboration."

James nodded, "By providing training, resources, and support, we can empower employees to identify and implement improvements in their work areas. By celebrating successes, recognizing contributions, and promoting a spirit of experimentation, we can create an environment where continuous improvement thrives."

Step 5: Monitor Performance and Adapt as Needed

Sarah concluded the discussion by highlighting the importance of monitoring performance and adapting as needed, "As we implement JIT, it's essential to monitor key performance indicators, track progress, and adapt our strategies based on feedback and results."

James nodded, "By regularly reviewing performance data, conducting audits, and soliciting feedback from stakeholders, we can identify areas for further improvement and make adjustments to our processes and systems as needed. This enables us to stay agile and responsive in a dynamic and competitive marketplace."

Conclusion: Embracing JIT Principles

As the strategy session concluded, Sarah and James encouraged the team to embrace JIT principles and embark on their journey towards operational excellence. "By assessing current processes, establishing pull systems, streamlining production processes, fostering a culture of continuous improvement, and monitoring performance, we can successfully implement JIT in our organization and achieve our goals of efficiency, quality, and customer satisfaction," Sarah said.

James nodded in agreement, "Let's commit ourselves to the JIT mindset, to delivering products with precision, efficiency, and quality. Together, we can optimize our processes, reduce waste, and create value for our customers."

The team left the strategy session feeling inspired and motivated, ready to embark on their JIT journey and drive positive change in their organization. With a clear roadmap for implementation, Aurora Electronics was well-equipped to achieve their goals and aspirations.

JIT and Supply Chain Management

In a meeting room at Aurora Electronics, Sarah Mitchell and James Thompson led a discussion on integrating Just-In-Time (JIT) principles into the organization's supply chain management processes. Surrounded by whiteboards filled with diagrams and charts depicting supply chain flows, the team eagerly brainstormed strategies to optimize their supply chain and enhance their JIT capabilities.

Sarah began, "Good afternoon, everyone. Today, we're going to explore how we can integrate Just-In-Time (JIT) principles into our supply chain management processes to achieve greater efficiency, responsiveness, and collaboration."

James added, "By embracing JIT principles such as pull systems, Kanban systems, and continuous improvement, we can streamline our supply chain, minimize lead times, and enhance our overall competitiveness in the marketplace. Let's discuss strategies for integrating JIT into our supply chain."

Integration of Pull Systems

Sarah highlighted the first strategy for integrating JIT into the supply chain, "One key aspect of JIT is the implementation of pull systems, where production is driven by customer demand rather than forecasted projections. This requires close collaboration with our suppliers to ensure that they can respond quickly to changes in demand."

James nodded, "By sharing demand forecasts, implementing vendor-managed inventory (VMI) systems, and establishing collaborative relationships with key suppliers, we can create a seamless flow of materials and components throughout our supply chain. This enables us to minimize inventory levels and reduce lead times while ensuring that we have the right materials available when needed."

Adoption of Kanban Systems

Sarah discussed the adoption of Kanban systems in the supply chain, "Kanban systems provide visual signals that trigger production and replenishment activities based on actual consumption. By implementing Kanban systems with our suppliers, we can improve communication, coordination, and synchronization of production and delivery schedules."

James elaborated, "By standardizing Kanban cards, establishing clear replenishment rules, and setting up electronic Kanban systems, we can streamline the flow of materials and information across our supply chain. This enables us to reduce the risk of stockouts, minimize excess inventory, and improve overall supply chain performance."

Continuous Improvement and Collaboration

Sarah emphasized the importance of continuous improvement and collaboration in the supply chain, "JIT is not just about optimizing individual processes but also about fostering collaboration and innovation throughout the supply chain. By engaging suppliers in our continuous improvement efforts and sharing best practices, we can drive mutual benefits and create a competitive advantage."

James nodded, "By establishing regular communication channels, conducting joint improvement projects, and sharing performance data with our suppliers, we can build trust, transparency, and accountability in our relationships. This enables us to identify opportunities for optimization, resolve issues proactively, and drive continuous improvement across the entire supply chain."

Conclusion: Leveraging JIT in Supply Chain Management

As the meeting concluded, Sarah and James encouraged the team to leverage JIT principles to enhance their supply chain management processes. "By integrating pull systems, Kanban systems, and continuous improvement into our supply chain, we can achieve greater efficiency, responsiveness, and collaboration," Sarah said.

James nodded in agreement, "Let's commit ourselves to the JIT mindset, to delivering value to our customers with precision, efficiency, and quality. Together, we can optimize our supply chain, reduce lead times, and create a competitive advantage in the marketplace."

The team left the meeting feeling inspired and motivated, ready to integrate JIT principles into their supply chain management processes and drive positive change throughout the organization. With a clear roadmap for integration, Aurora Electronics was well-positioned to achieve their goals of operational excellence and customer satisfaction.

Case Studies: JIT Success Stories

In the conference room at Aurora Electronics, Sarah Mitchell and James Thompson led a presentation showcasing case studies of Just-In-Time (JIT) success stories. With eager anticipation, employees gathered to learn from real-world examples of organizations that had successfully implemented JIT principles to drive positive change in their operations.

Sarah began, "Good morning, everyone. Today, we're going to explore case studies of organizations that have embraced Just-In-Time (JIT) principles and achieved remarkable results in their operations. These success stories serve as inspiring examples of the transformative power of JIT to drive efficiency, quality, and customer satisfaction."

James added, "By studying these case studies, we can gain valuable insights into how JIT principles have been applied in different contexts and industries, and how they can be adapted and implemented in our own organization. Let's dive in and explore these JIT success stories."

Case Study 1: Toyota Production System (TPS)

Sarah introduced the first case study, "Our first case study focuses on Toyota, the pioneer of JIT production and the creator of the Toyota Production System (TPS). Through the implementation of JIT principles such as pull systems, Kanban systems, and continuous improvement, Toyota revolutionized the automotive industry and set new standards for efficiency, quality, and innovation."

James elaborated, "By optimizing production flows, minimizing inventory levels, and empowering frontline employees to contribute to process improvement, Toyota achieved significant reductions in lead times, production costs, and defects. This enabled Toyota to deliver products with greater precision, reliability, and value, and establish itself as a global leader in the automotive industry."

Case Study 2: Dell Inc.

The next slide displayed a case study of Dell Inc., a pioneer in the computer manufacturing industry. "Our second case study examines how Dell leveraged JIT principles to transform its supply chain and revolutionize the computer manufacturing process," Sarah explained.

James shared, "By implementing build-to-order manufacturing, Dell minimized inventory levels, reduced lead times, and improved responsiveness to customer demand. By collaborating closely with suppliers and implementing JIT practices throughout its supply chain, Dell achieved greater flexibility, agility, and cost-effectiveness, enabling it to deliver customized products to customers with unprecedented speed and efficiency."

Case Study 3: Zara

The presentation shifted to a case study of Zara, a leading fashion retailer known for its fast-fashion business model. "Our third case study showcases how Zara embraced JIT principles to disrupt the fashion industry and redefine the concept of fast fashion," Sarah said.

James highlighted, "By implementing a highly responsive supply chain, leveraging real-time data and analytics, and adopting JIT practices such as quick response manufacturing and lean inventory management, Zara reduced lead times, minimized excess inventory, and accelerated time-to-market for its fashion collections. This enabled Zara to stay ahead of trends, meet customer demand with precision, and maintain a competitive edge in the fast-paced world of fashion."

Conclusion: Lessons Learned from JIT Success Stories

As the presentation concluded, Sarah and James summarized the key lessons learned from the JIT success stories. "These case studies demonstrate the transformative power of JIT to drive efficiency, quality, and customer satisfaction across a wide range of industries," Sarah said.

James nodded, "By studying these success stories, we can gain valuable insights into how JIT principles can be applied in our own organization to achieve similar results. Let's draw inspiration from these examples and leverage JIT to drive positive change and create value for our customers."

The audience left the conference room feeling inspired and motivated, ready to apply the insights gained from the JIT success stories to drive continuous improvement in their own processes and operations. With a clear understanding of the impact of JIT in action, Aurora Electronics was well-equipped to achieve their goals of operational excellence and customer satisfaction.

Challenges and Solutions in JIT Implementation

In a team meeting at Aurora Electronics, Sarah Mitchell and James Thompson led a discussion on the challenges and solutions in Just-In-Time (JIT) implementation. Surrounded by whiteboards filled with lists of challenges and proposed solutions, the team eagerly brainstormed strategies to overcome obstacles and drive successful JIT implementation.

Sarah began, "Good afternoon, everyone. Today, we're going to discuss the challenges we may encounter in implementing Just-In-Time (JIT) production in our organization and explore strategies to address them effectively."

James added, "By understanding the potential challenges and proactively addressing them, we can minimize risks, optimize our processes, and achieve greater success in our JIT implementation efforts. Let's dive in and explore the challenges and solutions in JIT implementation."

Challenge 1: Resistance to Change

Sarah highlighted the first challenge in JIT implementation, "One of the primary challenges we may encounter is resistance to change. Implementing JIT requires a shift in mindset, processes, and behaviors, which may be met with resistance from employees who are accustomed to traditional ways of working."

James nodded, "To address this challenge, it's essential to communicate the vision and benefits of JIT, involve employees in the change process, and provide training and support to help them adapt to new ways of working. By fostering a culture of openness, collaboration, and empowerment, we can overcome resistance to change and create buy-in for our JIT initiatives."

Challenge 2: Dependency on Suppliers

Sarah discussed the challenge of dependency on suppliers, "Another challenge we may face is dependency on suppliers for timely delivery of materials and components. Any disruptions or delays in the supply chain can have a significant impact on our ability to meet customer demand and maintain production schedules."

James added, "To mitigate this challenge, we can establish close relationships with key suppliers, implement vendor-managed inventory (VMI) systems, and diversify our supplier base to reduce the risk of dependency on a single source. By working collaboratively with suppliers and implementing JIT practices throughout the supply chain, we can improve reliability, responsiveness, and resilience."

Challenge 3: Variability in Demand

Sarah emphasized the challenge of variability in demand, "Variability in customer demand can pose challenges in JIT implementation, as it may lead to fluctuations in production schedules, inventory levels, and resource utilization. Without accurate forecasting and planning, we may struggle to align production with actual demand."

James nodded, "To address this challenge, we can implement demand forecasting tools, collaborate closely with customers to understand their needs and preferences, and adopt flexible production strategies such as mixed-model production and level scheduling. By being proactive in anticipating and responding to changes in demand, we can minimize disruptions and maximize efficiency in our operations."

Challenge 4: Quality Control

Sarah discussed the challenge of maintaining quality control in JIT production, "With JIT, there is little room for error, as defects or errors can disrupt production schedules and impact customer satisfaction. Maintaining stringent quality control measures is essential to ensure that products meet the highest standards of quality and reliability."

James added, "To overcome this challenge, we can implement robust quality management systems, establish clear quality standards and performance metrics, and provide training and support to employees to ensure compliance with quality requirements. By prioritizing quality at every stage of the production process, we can build trust and confidence with our customers and strengthen our competitive position in the marketplace."

Challenge 5: Inventory Management

Sarah highlighted the challenge of inventory management in JIT production, "With JIT, inventory levels are kept to a minimum, which requires precise inventory management to ensure that materials and components are available when needed without excess stockpiling."

James nodded, "To address this challenge, we can implement inventory control techniques such as Kanban systems, establish safety stock levels based on lead time variability and demand uncertainty, and leverage technology such as inventory management software to monitor and track inventory levels in real-time. By optimizing inventory management practices, we can minimize waste, reduce costs, and improve efficiency in our operations."

Conclusion: Overcoming Challenges in JIT Implementation

As the meeting concluded, Sarah and James summarized the key strategies for overcoming challenges in JIT implementation. "By addressing resistance to change, managing dependencies on suppliers, mitigating variability in demand, maintaining quality control, and optimizing inventory management, we can minimize risks and maximize the success of our JIT implementation efforts," Sarah said.

James nodded in agreement, "Let's work together to overcome these challenges and drive positive change in our organization. By embracing the JIT mindset and adopting proactive strategies, we can achieve our goals of operational excellence and customer satisfaction."

The team left the meeting feeling empowered and motivated, ready to tackle the challenges of JIT implementation head-on and drive successful outcomes in their operations. With a clear understanding of the potential obstacles and solutions, Aurora Electronics was well-equipped to navigate the complexities of JIT implementation and achieve their goals of efficiency, quality, and customer satisfaction.

7

Chapter 7: Lean Tools and Techniques

5S System: Sort, Set in Order, Shine, Standardize, Sustain

In a workshop at Aurora Electronics, Sarah Mitchell and James Thompson led a training session on the 5S System, a fundamental lean tool for workplace organization and efficiency. Surrounded by workbenches, tools, and equipment, employees eagerly gathered to learn about the principles and practices of 5S.

Sarah began, "Good morning, everyone. Today, we're going to explore the 5S System, a cornerstone of lean manufacturing that focuses on workplace organization, cleanliness, and standardization. By implementing the 5S principles of Sort, Set in Order, Shine, Standardize, and Sustain, we can create a more organized, efficient, and productive work environment."

James added, "By adopting the 5S System, we can improve safety, reduce waste, enhance quality, and increase productivity in our operations. Let's dive in and explore the principles and practices of 5S."

Sort:

Sarah introduced the first step of the 5S System, "The first step of 5S is Sort, which involves removing unnecessary items from the workplace and organizing items based on their necessity and frequency of use."

James elaborated, "By sorting through tools, materials, and equipment, we can eliminate clutter, reduce excess inventory, and create more space for productive activities. This enables us to streamline workflows, minimize waste, and improve overall efficiency in our operations."

Set in Order:

Sarah discussed the second step of the 5S System, "The second step of 5S is Set in Order, which involves organizing and arranging items in a systematic and ergonomic manner for easy access and retrieval."

James emphasized, "By establishing designated storage locations, labeling tools and materials, and implementing visual management techniques such as shadow boards and signage, we can create a more organized and efficient workspace. This enables us to reduce search times, minimize errors, and improve workflow continuity."

Shine:

Sarah introduced the third step of the 5S System, "The third step of 5S is Shine, which involves cleaning and maintaining the workplace to ensure a safe, hygienic, and productive environment."

James nodded, "By implementing regular cleaning schedules, conducting inspections, and addressing any safety hazards or maintenance issues promptly, we can create a culture of cleanliness and pride in our workplace. This not only improves morale and employee satisfaction but also enhances safety and quality in our operations."

Standardize:

Sarah discussed the fourth step of the 5S System, "The fourth step of 5S is Standardize, which involves establishing standardized work procedures and protocols to sustain the improvements made during the Sort, Set in Order, and Shine steps."

James elaborated, "By documenting best practices, creating visual work instructions, and training employees on standardized procedures, we can ensure consistency, reliability, and repeatability in our operations. This enables us to maintain high levels of performance and quality over time."

Sustain:

Sarah introduced the fifth and final step of the 5S System, "The fifth step of 5S is Sustain, which involves fostering a culture of continuous improvement and accountability to ensure that the gains achieved through the Sort, Set in Order, Shine, and Standardize steps are maintained over the long term."

James emphasized, "By engaging employees, encouraging participation, and recognizing achievements, we can sustain the momentum of improvement and continuously strive for excellence in our operations. This enables us to adapt to changing conditions, overcome challenges, and achieve our goals of efficiency, quality, and customer satisfaction."

Conclusion: Embracing the 5S System

As the training session concluded, Sarah and James encouraged the team to embrace the principles and practices of the 5S System in their daily work. "By implementing Sort, Set in Order, Shine, Standardize, and Sustain in our workplace, we can create a more organized, efficient, and productive environment," Sarah said.

James nodded in agreement, "Let's commit ourselves to the 5S mindset, to creating a workplace that is safe, clean, and conducive to high-performance work. Together, we can achieve our goals of operational excellence and customer satisfaction."

The team left the workshop feeling inspired and motivated, ready to implement the principles of the 5S System and drive positive change in their workplace. With a clear understanding of the 5S principles and practices, Aurora Electronics was well-equipped to achieve their goals of efficiency, quality, and continuous improvement.

Kanban System

On the bustling production floor of Aurora Electronics, Sarah Mitchell and James Thompson led a hands-on demonstration of the Kanban System, a powerful lean tool for inventory management and production control. Surrounded by conveyor belts, workstations, and inventory racks, employees eagerly gathered to learn about the principles and practices of Kanban.

Sarah began, "Good afternoon, everyone. Today, we're going to explore the Kanban System, a key lean tool for managing inventory, controlling production, and optimizing workflow. By implementing Kanban, we can create a more efficient, responsive, and synchronized production process."

James added, "By visualizing workflow, limiting work in progress, and aligning production with customer demand, Kanban enables us to minimize waste, reduce lead times, and improve overall efficiency in our operations. Let's dive in and explore the principles and practices of the Kanban System."

Introduction to Kanban:

Sarah introduced the concept of Kanban, "Kanban is a Japanese term that means 'visual card' or 'signal.' It originated in the Toyota Production System (TPS) as a way to control inventory levels and production flow."

James elaborated, "Kanban uses visual signals, such as cards or bins, to trigger production and replenishment activities based on actual consumption. By linking production directly to customer demand, Kanban helps us avoid overproduction, minimize inventory levels, and respond quickly to changes in demand."

Types of Kanban:

Sarah discussed the different types of Kanban used in manufacturing, "There are two primary types of Kanban: production Kanban and withdrawal Kanban."

James explained, "Production Kanban authorizes the production of a specific quantity of parts or products in response to a customer order or signal from downstream processes. Withdrawal Kanban, on the other hand, authorizes the movement of parts or products from one process to the next."

Kanban Board Setup:

Sarah led the team through the setup of a Kanban board, "A Kanban board is a visual management tool that provides a real-time view of workflow and inventory levels."

James demonstrated, "By dividing the board into columns representing different stages of production and using cards or bins to represent work items, we can track progress, identify bottlenecks, and ensure smooth flow throughout the production process."

Benefits of Kanban:

Sarah discussed the benefits of implementing Kanban, "By visualizing workflow, limiting work in progress, and aligning production with customer demand, Kanban enables us to achieve several key benefits."

James elaborated, "These benefits include reduced lead times, improved on-time delivery performance, increased flexibility, and enhanced overall efficiency in our operations. By optimizing production flow and minimizing waste, Kanban helps us deliver value to our customers with greater precision and reliability."

Conclusion: Embracing the Kanban System

As the demonstration concluded, Sarah and James encouraged the team to embrace the principles and practices of the Kanban System in their daily work. "By implementing Kanban, we can create a more efficient, responsive, and synchronized production process," Sarah said.

James nodded in agreement, "Let's commit ourselves to the Kanban mindset, to visualizing workflow, limiting work in progress, and aligning production with customer demand. Together, we can achieve our goals of efficiency, quality, and customer satisfaction."

The team left the production floor feeling empowered and motivated, ready to implement the principles of the Kanban System and drive positive change in their operations. With a clear understanding of Kanban principles and practices, Aurora Electronics was well-equipped to achieve their goals of operational excellence and customer satisfaction.

Poka-Yoke (Error Proofing)

In the Quality Control Lab at Aurora Electronics, Sarah Mitchell and James Thompson led a training session on Poka-Yoke, a crucial lean tool for error proofing and quality improvement. Surrounded by testing equipment, inspection stations, and quality control charts, employees gathered eagerly to learn about the principles and practices of Poka-Yoke.

Sarah began, "Good morning, everyone. Today, we're going to explore Poka-Yoke, a powerful lean tool for error prevention and quality improvement. By implementing Poka-Yoke techniques, we can minimize defects, reduce rework, and ensure that our products meet the highest standards of quality and reliability."

James added, "Poka-Yoke, which translates to 'mistake-proofing' in Japanese, focuses on designing processes and systems in such a way that errors are impossible or immediately detected and corrected. Let's dive in and explore the principles and practices of Poka-Yoke."

Introduction to Poka-Yoke:

Sarah introduced the concept of Poka-Yoke, "Poka-Yoke is based on the principle that it is far more effective to prevent errors from occurring in the first place than to detect and correct them later."

James elaborated, "Poka-Yoke techniques involve designing foolproof mechanisms, devices, or procedures that prevent errors from happening or make them immediately visible and easily corrected. By eliminating human error and variability, Poka-Yoke helps us achieve consistent and reliable results in our operations."

Types of Poka-Yoke:

Sarah discussed the different types of Poka-Yoke techniques used in manufacturing, "There are two primary types of Poka-Yoke: prevention-based and detection-based."

James explained, "Prevention-based Poka-Yoke focuses on designing processes or systems in such a way that errors are impossible to make. Detection-based Poka-Yoke, on the other hand, involves implementing checks or sensors to detect errors as they occur and trigger corrective actions."

Examples of Poka-Yoke:

Sarah led the team through examples of Poka-Yoke techniques in various industries, "Poka-Yoke techniques can take many forms, from simple to complex, depending on the nature of the error and the context of the process."

James demonstrated, "Examples of Poka-Yoke include foolproof jigs and fixtures, mistake-proofing sensors and alarms, and error-proofing checklists and procedures. By implementing Poka-Yoke techniques, we can eliminate defects, improve process reliability, and enhance overall quality in our operations."

Benefits of Poka-Yoke:

Sarah discussed the benefits of implementing Poka-Yoke, "By preventing errors from occurring or making them immediately visible and easily corrected, Poka-Yoke enables us to achieve several key benefits."

James elaborated, "These benefits include reduced rework and scrap, improved product quality and reliability, increased productivity, and enhanced customer satisfaction. By embedding quality into our processes and systems, Poka-Yoke helps us deliver defect-free products to our customers with greater confidence and consistency."

Conclusion: Embracing Poka-Yoke

As the training session concluded, Sarah and James encouraged the team to embrace the principles and practices of Poka-Yoke in their daily work. "By implementing Poka-Yoke, we can minimize defects, reduce rework, and ensure that our products meet the highest standards of quality and reliability," Sarah said.

James nodded in agreement, "Let's commit ourselves to the Poka-Yoke mindset, to designing foolproof processes and systems that prevent errors from occurring or make them immediately visible and easily corrected. Together, we can achieve our goals of operational excellence and customer satisfaction."

The team left the Quality Control Lab feeling inspired and motivated, ready to implement the principles of Poka-Yoke and drive positive change in their operations. With a clear understanding of Poka-Yoke techniques, Aurora Electronics was well-equipped to achieve their goals of error-proofing and quality improvement.

Total Productive Maintenance (TPM)

In the heart of the Aurora Electronics manufacturing plant, Sarah Mitchell and James Thompson led a training session on Total Productive Maintenance (TPM), a vital lean tool for maximizing equipment reliability and efficiency. Surrounded by humming machinery, maintenance tools, and equipment manuals, employees gathered eagerly to learn about the principles and practices of TPM.

Sarah began, "Good morning, everyone. Today, we're going to explore Total Productive Maintenance (TPM), a key lean tool for optimizing equipment performance, minimizing downtime, and maximizing overall productivity. By implementing TPM, we can ensure that our equipment operates at peak efficiency and supports our goals of operational excellence and customer satisfaction."

James added, "TPM focuses on empowering operators to take ownership of equipment maintenance, conducting proactive maintenance activities, and continuously improving equipment reliability and performance. Let's dive in and explore the principles and practices of TPM."

Introduction to TPM:

Sarah introduced the concept of TPM, "TPM is based on the principle that equipment reliability is essential for achieving operational excellence and delivering value to customers."

James elaborated, "TPM aims to eliminate equipment-related losses by engaging operators in proactive maintenance activities, conducting routine inspections and cleaning, and implementing measures to prevent breakdowns and defects. By maximizing equipment uptime and performance, TPM helps us achieve higher levels of productivity and efficiency in our operations."

Eight Pillars of TPM:

Sarah discussed the eight pillars of TPM, "TPM is structured around eight pillars, each focusing on different aspects of equipment maintenance and performance improvement."

James explained, "These pillars include autonomous maintenance, planned maintenance, focused improvement, early equipment management, quality maintenance, training and education, administrative and office TPM, and safety, health, and environment. By addressing each of these pillars, we can create a comprehensive TPM program that drives continuous improvement and excellence in our operations."

Implementation of TPM:

Sarah led the team through the implementation of TPM principles, "Implementing TPM involves several key steps, including establishing a cross-functional TPM team, conducting equipment audits and assessments, and developing comprehensive maintenance plans."

James demonstrated, "By involving operators in equipment care and maintenance, providing training and support, and implementing visual management techniques such as TPM boards and charts, we can create a culture of ownership, accountability, and continuous improvement. This enables us to identify and address equipment issues proactively, minimize downtime, and optimize overall equipment effectiveness (OEE)."

Benefits of TPM:

Sarah discussed the benefits of implementing TPM, "By maximizing equipment reliability and performance, TPM enables us to achieve several key benefits."

James elaborated, "These benefits include reduced downtime, increased equipment availability, improved product quality, higher productivity, and lower maintenance costs. By optimizing equipment performance and minimizing losses, TPM helps us achieve our goals of operational excellence and customer satisfaction."

Conclusion: Embracing TPM

As the training session concluded, Sarah and James encouraged the team to embrace the principles and practices of TPM in their daily work. "By implementing TPM, we can ensure that our equipment operates at peak efficiency and supports our goals of operational excellence and customer satisfaction,"

Sarah said.

James nodded in agreement, "Let's commit ourselves to the TPM mindset, to empowering operators, maximizing equipment reliability, and driving continuous improvement in our operations. Together, we can achieve our goals and deliver value to our customers."

The team left the training session feeling inspired and motivated, ready to implement the principles of TPM and drive positive change in their operations. With a clear understanding of TPM principles and practices, Aurora Electronics was well-equipped to achieve their goals of equipment reliability and operational excellence.

SMED (Single-Minute Exchange of Dies)

In the heart of the production line at Aurora Electronics, Sarah Mitchell and James Thompson led a training session on SMED (Single-Minute Exchange of Dies), a critical lean tool for reducing setup times and increasing operational flexibility. Surrounded by machinery, tooling stations, and production schedules, employees gathered eagerly to learn about the principles and practices of SMED.

Sarah began, "Good morning, everyone. Today, we're going to explore SMED, a powerful lean tool for reducing setup times and enabling quick and efficient changeovers between production runs. By implementing SMED techniques, we can increase operational flexibility, minimize downtime, and respond more effectively to customer demand."

James added, "SMED focuses on streamlining setup procedures, standardizing work processes, and eliminating non-essential activities to achieve rapid and efficient changeovers.

Let's dive in and explore the principles and practices of SMED."

Introduction to SMED:

Sarah introduced the concept of SMED, "SMED originated from the Toyota Production System (TPS) and is based on the principle that reducing setup times is essential for achieving higher levels of productivity and flexibility in manufacturing."

James elaborated, "SMED aims to convert as much setup time as possible from external (performed while the equipment is stopped) to internal (performed while the equipment is running). By reducing setup times and increasing equipment availability, SMED helps us achieve faster changeovers and greater responsiveness to customer demand."

Steps for SMED Implementation:

Sarah led the team through the steps for implementing SMED techniques, "Implementing SMED involves several key steps, including conducting a setup time analysis, separating internal and external setup activities, and converting external setup activities to internal ones."

James demonstrated, "By standardizing setup procedures, creating setup checklists, and implementing parallel setup activities, we can reduce setup times and improve overall efficiency in our operations. This enables us to change over between production runs quickly and efficiently, minimizing downtime and maximizing productivity."

Examples of SMED Techniques:

Sarah discussed examples of SMED techniques used in various industries, "SMED techniques can take many forms, depending on the nature of the setup and the equipment involved."

James explained, "Examples of SMED techniques include

pre-staging tools and materials, using quick-release fasteners and fixtures, and creating standardized setup procedures and checklists. By applying these techniques, we can reduce setup times to single-digit minutes or even seconds, enabling us to achieve rapid changeovers and meet customer demand with greater agility and efficiency."

Benefits of SMED:

Sarah discussed the benefits of implementing SMED, "By reducing setup times and enabling quick changeovers, SMED enables us to achieve several key benefits."

James elaborated, "These benefits include increased equipment utilization, reduced lead times, improved flexibility, and enhanced responsiveness to customer demand. By streamlining setup procedures and eliminating waste, SMED helps us achieve our goals of operational excellence and customer satisfaction."

Conclusion: Embracing SMED

As the training session concluded, Sarah and James encouraged the team to embrace the principles and practices of SMED in their daily work. "By implementing SMED, we can reduce setup times and increase operational flexibility, enabling us to respond more effectively to customer demand," Sarah said.

James nodded in agreement, "Let's commit ourselves to the SMED mindset, to streamlining setup procedures, reducing waste, and achieving rapid changeovers in our operations. Together, we can achieve our goals and deliver value to our customers."

The team left the training session feeling inspired and motivated, ready to implement the principles of SMED and drive positive change in their operations. With a clear understanding of SMED techniques, Aurora Electronics was well-equipped to achieve their goals of setup time reduction and operational flexibility.

Value Stream Mapping

In the conference room at Aurora Electronics, Sarah Mitchell and James Thompson led a training session on Value Stream Mapping (VSM), a crucial lean tool for visualizing and improving workflow processes. Surrounded by whiteboards, markers, and process diagrams, employees gathered eagerly to learn about the principles and practices of VSM.

Sarah began, "Good morning, everyone. Today, we're going to explore Value Stream Mapping, a powerful lean tool for identifying waste, streamlining processes, and optimizing workflow. By implementing VSM techniques, we can gain valuable insights into our operations and drive continuous improvement."

James added, "VSM focuses on mapping the flow of materials and information from supplier to customer, identifying value-added and non-value-added activities, and visualizing opportunities for improvement. Let's dive in and explore the principles and practices of VSM."

Introduction to Value Stream Mapping:
Sarah introduced the concept of Value Stream Mapping, "Value Stream Mapping is a visual representation of all the steps required to deliver a product or service from start to finish, including both value-added and non-value-added activities."

James elaborated, "VSM enables us to see the big picture of our processes, identify bottlenecks and waste, and develop action plans for improvement. By creating a visual map of our value streams, we can align our efforts with customer needs, improve flow, and enhance overall efficiency in our operations."

Steps for Value Stream Mapping:

Sarah led the team through the steps for conducting Value Stream Mapping, "Conducting VSM involves several key steps, including selecting a value stream to map, gathering data on current processes, and creating a current state map."

James demonstrated, "By analyzing the current state map, identifying waste and opportunities for improvement, and developing a future state map, we can create a roadmap for achieving our goals of operational excellence and customer satisfaction. This enables us to prioritize improvement projects and allocate resources effectively."

Examples of Value Stream Mapping:

Sarah discussed examples of Value Stream Mapping in various industries, "VSM can be applied to any process or workflow, from manufacturing to service industries."

James explained, "Examples of VSM include mapping the flow of materials and information in a manufacturing plant, mapping the patient journey in a healthcare facility, or mapping the order-to-delivery process in a retail operation. By visualizing value streams and identifying opportunities for improvement, VSM helps us achieve our goals of efficiency, quality, and customer satisfaction."

Benefits of Value Stream Mapping:

Sarah discussed the benefits of implementing Value Stream Mapping, "By visualizing workflow, identifying waste, and developing action plans for improvement, VSM enables us to achieve several key benefits."

James elaborated, "These benefits include reduced lead times, improved flow, increased productivity, and enhanced customer satisfaction. By aligning our efforts with customer needs and focusing on value-added activities, VSM helps us deliver products and services more efficiently and effectively."

Conclusion: Embracing Value Stream Mapping

As the training session concluded, Sarah and James encouraged the team to embrace the principles and practices of Value Stream Mapping in their daily work. "By implementing VSM, we can gain valuable insights into our operations and drive continuous improvement," Sarah said.

James nodded in agreement, "Let's commit ourselves to the VSM mindset, to visualizing workflow, identifying waste, and developing action plans for improvement. Together, we can achieve our goals and deliver value to our customers."

The team left the conference room feeling inspired and motivated, ready to implement the principles of Value Stream Mapping and drive positive change in their operations. With a clear understanding of VSM techniques, Aurora Electronics was well-equipped to achieve their goals of process optimization and operational excellence.

8

Chapter 8: Lean Leadership and Culture

Characteristics of Lean Leaders

In the executive boardroom at Aurora Electronics, Sarah Mitchell and James Thompson led a discussion on the characteristics of lean leaders, essential for fostering a culture of continuous improvement and operational excellence. Surrounded by sleek furniture, a polished conference table, and panoramic views of the city skyline, executives and managers gathered eagerly to learn about the principles and practices of lean leadership.

Sarah began, "Good morning, everyone. Today, we're going to explore the characteristics of lean leaders, those individuals who inspire and guide their teams toward operational excellence and continuous improvement. By embodying these characteristics, we can create a culture of accountability, innovation, and teamwork."

James added, "Lean leaders serve as role models, mentors,

and catalysts for change. They demonstrate a commitment to continuous learning, a focus on customer value, and a dedication to empowering their teams. Let's dive in and explore the characteristics of lean leaders."

Characteristics of Lean Leaders:

Sarah introduced the key characteristics of lean leaders, "Lean leaders possess several key attributes that distinguish them as champions of continuous improvement and operational excellence."

James elaborated, "These characteristics include:

1. **Visionary Leadership:** Lean leaders have a clear vision of where they want to take their organization and inspire others to follow.
2. **Commitment to Continuous Improvement:** Lean leaders are lifelong learners who are committed to seeking out new ideas, challenging the status quo, and driving innovation.
3. **Customer Focus:** Lean leaders prioritize the needs and preferences of customers, aligning their strategies and actions to deliver value and exceed expectations.
4. **Empowerment and Accountability:** Lean leaders empower their teams to take ownership of their work, providing support, resources, and recognition, while also holding them accountable for results.
5. **Effective Communication:** Lean leaders communicate openly, honestly, and transparently, fostering a culture of trust, collaboration, and engagement.
6. **Resilience and Adaptability:** Lean leaders are resilient in the face of challenges and adaptable to change, maintaining a positive attitude and seeking opportunities for

growth and development.
7. **Lead by Example:** Lean leaders lead by example, demonstrating the behaviors and attitudes they expect from their teams, and consistently modeling the principles of lean thinking and continuous improvement."

Case Studies: Exemplary Lean Leaders

Sarah presented case studies of exemplary lean leaders from various industries, "Let's take a look at some real-world examples of lean leaders who have successfully implemented lean principles and practices in their organizations."

James shared, "One such example is John Smith, CEO of XYZ Manufacturing, who transformed his company's culture by championing lean thinking and empowering his teams to identify and eliminate waste. Under his leadership, XYZ Manufacturing achieved significant improvements in productivity, quality, and customer satisfaction."

Conclusion: Embracing Lean Leadership

As the discussion concluded, Sarah and James encouraged the executives and managers to embody the characteristics of lean leaders in their daily leadership practices. "By embodying these characteristics, we can create a culture of continuous improvement and operational excellence," Sarah said.

James nodded in agreement, "Let's commit ourselves to the principles of lean leadership, to vision, commitment, empowerment, and accountability. Together, we can inspire our teams to achieve greatness and deliver value to our customers."

The executives and managers left the boardroom feeling inspired and motivated, ready to embody the characteristics of lean leaders and drive positive change in their organization.

With a clear understanding of lean leadership principles, Aurora Electronics was well-equipped to achieve their goals of operational excellence and customer satisfaction.

Developing Lean Leadership Skills

In the training room at Aurora Electronics, Sarah Mitchell and James Thompson facilitated a workshop on developing lean leadership skills, essential for driving continuous improvement and fostering a culture of operational excellence. Surrounded by flip charts, training materials, and interactive exercises, managers and team leaders gathered eagerly to enhance their leadership capabilities.

Sarah began, "Good afternoon, everyone. Today, we're going to focus on developing lean leadership skills, equipping ourselves with the tools and techniques necessary to lead our teams toward continuous improvement and success. By honing these skills, we can inspire and empower our teams to achieve their full potential."

James added, "Developing lean leadership skills is an ongoing process that requires self-awareness, practice, and commitment to growth. Let's dive in and explore how we can develop and strengthen our leadership capabilities."

Developing Lean Leadership Skills:

Sarah introduced the key areas for developing lean leadership skills, "Developing lean leadership skills involves focusing on several key areas that are essential for driving continuous improvement and fostering a culture of operational excellence."

James elaborated, "These areas include:

1. **Self-Awareness:** Lean leaders cultivate self-awareness by reflecting on their strengths, weaknesses, and areas for growth. They seek feedback from others, engage in continuous learning, and strive to become better leaders each day.
2. **Communication:** Effective communication is crucial for lean leaders. They communicate openly, honestly, and transparently, actively listening to others, providing feedback, and fostering collaboration and teamwork.
3. **Problem-Solving:** Lean leaders are skilled problem-solvers who approach challenges with curiosity, creativity, and resilience. They encourage their teams to identify root causes, generate innovative solutions, and implement sustainable improvements.
4. **Decision-Making:** Lean leaders make informed decisions based on data, facts, and input from stakeholders. They consider the long-term impact of their decisions, weigh risks and opportunities, and take decisive action when necessary.
5. **Empowerment and Delegation:** Lean leaders empower their teams to take ownership of their work, providing support, resources, and guidance while allowing autonomy and accountability. They delegate tasks effectively, leveraging the strengths and talents of their team members.
6. **Coaching and Development:** Lean leaders are committed to the growth and development of their team members. They provide mentorship, coaching, and opportunities for learning and skill-building, helping their teams reach their full potential.
7. **Leading by Example:** Lean leaders lead by example,

demonstrating the behaviors and attitudes they expect from their teams. They embody the principles of lean thinking and continuous improvement, inspiring others to follow their lead."

Interactive Exercises:

Sarah and James facilitated interactive exercises and role-playing scenarios to practice and reinforce lean leadership skills. Participants engaged in team-building activities, problem-solving exercises, and communication challenges, applying lean principles and techniques to real-world scenarios.

Conclusion: Strengthening Lean Leadership Skills

As the workshop concluded, Sarah and James encouraged the managers and team leaders to apply the skills and techniques they had learned to their daily leadership practices. "By developing and strengthening our lean leadership skills, we can inspire and empower our teams to achieve greatness," Sarah said.

James nodded in agreement, "Let's commit ourselves to continuous learning, growth, and improvement as lean leaders. Together, we can drive positive change and foster a culture of operational excellence in our organization."

The managers and team leaders left the training room feeling energized and equipped with the tools and techniques necessary to lead their teams toward continuous improvement and success. With a renewed focus on developing lean leadership skills, Aurora Electronics was well-positioned to achieve its goals of operational excellence and customer satisfaction.

Building a Lean Culture

In the bustling town hall of Aurora Electronics, Sarah Mitchell and James Thompson convened a meeting to discuss the importance of building a lean culture, essential for driving continuous improvement and operational excellence. Surrounded by employees from all departments, gathered in rows of chairs, Sarah and James stood at the front of the room, ready to inspire and empower their colleagues.

Sarah began, "Good afternoon, everyone. Today, we're going to focus on building a lean culture, creating an environment where continuous improvement is not just a goal but a way of life. By fostering a lean culture, we can unlock the full potential of our organization and achieve excellence in everything we do."

James added, "Building a lean culture requires commitment, collaboration, and a shared vision of success. Let's dive in and explore how we can create a culture of continuous improvement and operational excellence together."

Building a Lean Culture:

Sarah introduced the key elements for building a lean culture, "Building a lean culture involves fostering an environment where continuous improvement is ingrained in our values, behaviors, and processes."

James elaborated, "These elements include:

1. **Vision and Purpose:** A lean culture starts with a clear vision and purpose, articulated by senior leadership and communicated throughout the organization. It's about creating a shared understanding of why we do what we do and how we can improve together.

2. **Leadership Commitment:** Building a lean culture requires unwavering commitment from leaders at all levels of the organization. Leaders must lead by example, championing lean principles and practices, and actively supporting and empowering their teams.
3. **Employee Engagement:** A lean culture thrives on the engagement and involvement of every employee. It's about creating a culture where everyone feels valued, respected, and empowered to contribute their ideas and insights to drive improvement.
4. **Continuous Learning:** Learning is at the heart of a lean culture. It's about fostering a mindset of curiosity, experimentation, and growth, where every challenge is seen as an opportunity to learn and improve.
5. **Process Improvement:** Process improvement is the backbone of a lean culture. It's about identifying waste, streamlining processes, and driving efficiency and effectiveness in everything we do.
6. **Open Communication:** Open communication is essential for building trust, transparency, and collaboration within the organization. It's about creating a culture where feedback is welcomed, ideas are shared freely, and everyone feels heard and valued.
7. **Celebrating Success:** Celebrating success is vital for reinforcing the values and behaviors of a lean culture. It's about recognizing and rewarding achievements, both big and small, and celebrating the collective efforts of teams and individuals."

Interactive Discussion:

Sarah and James facilitated an interactive discussion with

employees, inviting them to share their thoughts, ideas, and experiences on building a lean culture. Employees shared success stories, challenges, and suggestions for creating a culture of continuous improvement and operational excellence.

Conclusion: Embracing a Lean Culture

As the meeting concluded, Sarah and James encouraged employees to embrace the principles and practices of lean thinking in their daily work. "By building a lean culture, we can unlock the full potential of our organization and achieve excellence in everything we do," Sarah said.

James nodded in agreement, "Let's commit ourselves to creating a culture where continuous improvement is not just a goal but a way of life. Together, we can build a lean culture that drives positive change and delivers value to our customers."

The employees left the town hall feeling inspired and motivated, ready to embrace the principles of lean thinking and contribute to building a culture of continuous improvement and operational excellence at Aurora Electronics. With a collective focus on building a lean culture, Aurora Electronics was well-positioned to achieve its goals and drive success in the future.

Engaging Employees in Lean Initiatives

In the vibrant workshop space at Aurora Electronics, Sarah Mitchell and James Thompson facilitated an employee engagement workshop focused on involving employees in lean initiatives. Surrounded by colorful posters, collaborative workstations, and a buzz of excitement, employees from various departments gathered, eager to contribute to the organization's continuous improvement efforts.

Sarah began, "Good morning, everyone. Today, we're going to explore how we can engage employees in lean initiatives, harnessing the collective knowledge, skills, and creativity of our team to drive positive change and achieve operational excellence. By involving employees in lean initiatives, we can create a culture of ownership, collaboration, and continuous improvement."

James added, "Engaging employees in lean initiatives is essential for fostering a sense of ownership, building trust, and driving sustainable improvement. Let's dive in and explore how we can involve employees in lean initiatives effectively."

Engaging Employees in Lean Initiatives:

Sarah introduced the key strategies for engaging employees in lean initiatives, "Engaging employees in lean initiatives involves creating opportunities for involvement, empowerment, and recognition."

James elaborated, "These strategies include:

1. **Training and Education:** Providing employees with the necessary training and education on lean principles and tools empowers them to actively participate in improvement initiatives and contribute valuable insights and ideas.
2. **Empowerment:** Empowering employees to identify and solve problems in their work areas fosters a sense of ownership and accountability. By involving employees in decision-making and problem-solving processes, we tap into their expertise and creativity.
3. **Continuous Improvement Teams:** Establishing cross-functional teams dedicated to continuous improvement

allows employees to collaborate, share ideas, and drive change collectively. These teams can identify opportunities for improvement, develop action plans, and monitor progress toward goals.
4. **Kaizen Events:** Conducting Kaizen events provides employees with focused opportunities to address specific challenges and implement rapid improvements. These events promote teamwork, innovation, and problem-solving skills among participants.
5. **Visual Management:** Using visual management techniques, such as performance boards, helps employees understand their role in achieving organizational goals, track progress, and celebrate successes.
6. **Recognition and Rewards:** Recognizing and rewarding employees for their contributions to lean initiatives reinforces a culture of engagement and commitment. Acknowledging individual and team achievements motivates employees to continue their efforts and inspires others to get involved."

Interactive Workshop:
Sarah and James facilitated an interactive workshop where employees participated in group activities, brainstorming sessions, and problem-solving exercises. Employees collaborated to identify areas for improvement, develop action plans, and share best practices for engaging in lean initiatives.

Conclusion: Empowering Employees in Lean Initiatives

As the workshop concluded, Sarah and James encouraged employees to apply the strategies and techniques they had learned to their daily work. "By engaging employees in lean initiatives, we can harness the collective expertise and creativity of our team to drive positive change and achieve operational excellence," Sarah said.

James nodded in agreement, "Let's empower each other to take ownership of our work, collaborate effectively, and drive continuous improvement. Together, we can make a meaningful impact on our organization and deliver value to our customers."

The employees left the workshop feeling energized and motivated, ready to actively participate in lean initiatives and contribute to the organization's success. With a renewed focus on engaging employees in lean initiatives, Aurora Electronics was well-positioned to achieve its goals of continuous improvement and operational excellence.

Case Studies: Lean Leadership in Action

In the conference room at Aurora Electronics, Sarah Mitchell and James Thompson presented case studies showcasing examples of lean leadership in action. Surrounded by charts, graphs, and presentations, managers and executives gathered eagerly, ready to learn from real-world examples of successful lean leadership.

Sarah began, "Good afternoon, everyone. Today, we're going to explore case studies of lean leadership in action, highlighting organizations that have successfully implemented lean principles and practices to drive continuous improvement and achieve operational excellence. By examining these case studies, we can gain valuable insights into the strategies and techniques used by exemplary lean leaders."

James added, "Case studies provide us with tangible examples of how lean leadership principles can be applied in diverse organizational settings. Let's dive in and explore these case studies together."

Case Study 1: Toyota

Sarah presented the first case study, "Toyota is widely regarded as a pioneer in lean manufacturing and a prime example of lean leadership in action. Through its Toyota Production System (TPS), Toyota has achieved remarkable success in driving continuous improvement, eliminating waste, and delivering value to customers."

James elaborated, "Key aspects of Toyota's lean leadership include a relentless focus on customer value, a commitment to employee empowerment and development, and a culture of continuous learning and improvement. By engaging employees at all levels of the organization, Toyota has been able to sustain its leadership position in the automotive industry and set the standard for lean manufacturing worldwide."

Case Study 2: Amazon

Sarah introduced the second case study, "Amazon, the e-commerce giant, has also demonstrated exemplary lean leadership in its operations. Through its relentless pursuit of operational excellence and customer-centricity, Amazon has revolutionized the retail industry and set new standards for efficiency and innovation."

James explained, "Amazon's lean leadership is characterized by its customer obsession, commitment to innovation, and relentless focus on eliminating waste and inefficiency. Through initiatives such as Prime delivery, fulfillment centers optimization, and continuous experimentation, Amazon has been able to continuously improve its operations and deliver exceptional value to customers around the world."

Case Study 3: Southwest Airlines

Sarah presented the third case study, "Southwest Airlines is another example of lean leadership in action. Through its focus on simplicity, efficiency, and employee engagement, Southwest has become one of the most successful and admired airlines in the world."

James elaborated, "Southwest's lean leadership is evident in its streamlined operations, employee-centric culture, and relentless pursuit of cost savings and operational efficiency. By empowering employees to make decisions, fostering a culture of teamwork and collaboration, and continuously improving its processes, Southwest has been able to thrive in a highly competitive industry and deliver exceptional value to its customers."

Conclusion: Learning from Exemplary Lean Leaders

As the presentation concluded, Sarah and James encouraged the managers and executives to reflect on the key lessons learned from the case studies. "By studying these examples of lean leadership in action, we can gain valuable insights into the strategies and techniques used by exemplary lean leaders to drive continuous improvement and achieve operational excellence," Sarah said.

James nodded in agreement, "Let's apply these lessons to our own leadership practices and organizational initiatives, striving to embody the principles of lean leadership in everything we do. Together, we can drive positive change and achieve greatness."

The managers and executives left the conference room feeling inspired and motivated, ready to apply the lessons learned from the case studies to their own leadership practices and organizational initiatives. With a renewed focus on lean leadership, Aurora Electronics was well-positioned to achieve its goals of continuous improvement and operational excellence.

Sustaining a Lean Culture

In the strategy session at Aurora Electronics, Sarah Mitchell and James Thompson led a discussion on sustaining a lean culture, vital for maintaining the organization's commitment to continuous improvement and operational excellence. Surrounded by whiteboards filled with diagrams, charts, and action plans, executives and managers gathered eagerly, ready to explore strategies for embedding lean principles into the fabric of the organization.

Sarah began, "Good morning, everyone. Today, we're going to focus on sustaining a lean culture, ensuring that our commitment to continuous improvement remains strong and resilient over time. By embedding lean principles into our culture, processes, and systems, we can create a foundation for long-term success and growth."

James added, "Sustaining a lean culture requires ongoing effort, vigilance, and reinforcement. Let's dive in and explore how we can sustain our commitment to continuous improvement and operational excellence."

Sustaining a Lean Culture:

Sarah introduced the key strategies for sustaining a lean culture, "Sustaining a lean culture involves embedding lean principles into every aspect of our organization, from leadership practices to daily operations."

James elaborated, "These strategies include:

1. **Leadership Commitment:** Sustaining a lean culture starts with unwavering commitment from leaders at all levels of the organization. Leaders must demonstrate their commitment to continuous improvement through their actions, decisions, and behaviors.
2. **Employee Engagement:** Engaging employees in lean initiatives and decision-making processes fosters a sense of ownership and accountability. By involving employees in setting goals, solving problems, and making improvements, we ensure their continued commitment to lean principles.
3. **Continuous Learning:** Learning is at the heart of a lean culture. We must provide ongoing training and development opportunities to ensure that employees have the knowledge and skills they need to drive continuous improvement.
4. **Process Improvement:** Process improvement is the lifeblood of a lean culture. We must continually identify and eliminate waste, streamline processes, and improve efficiency and effectiveness in everything we do.
5. **Open Communication:** Open communication is essential for sustaining a lean culture. We must create an environment where feedback is welcomed, ideas are shared freely, and everyone feels heard and valued.
6. **Recognition and Rewards:** Recognizing and rewarding employees for their contributions to lean initiatives reinforces a culture of engagement and commitment. Celebrating successes, both big and small, motivates employees to continue their efforts and inspires others to get involved.

Action Planning:

Sarah and James facilitated an action planning session where executives and managers worked together to develop strategies and action plans for sustaining a lean culture. Participants identified key initiatives, set goals, and assigned responsibilities to ensure accountability and progress.

Conclusion: Sustaining Lean Excellence

As the strategy session concluded, Sarah and James encouraged the executives and managers to implement the strategies and action plans developed during the session. "By sustaining our commitment to continuous improvement and operational excellence, we can achieve our goals and drive success in the long term," Sarah said.

James nodded in agreement, "Let's commit ourselves to embedding lean principles into our culture, processes, and systems, ensuring that our organization remains agile, adaptable, and resilient in the face of change. Together, we can sustain lean excellence and achieve greatness."

The executives and managers left the strategy session feeling motivated and empowered, ready to implement the strategies and action plans developed during the session. With a renewed focus on sustaining a lean culture, Aurora Electronics was well-positioned to achieve its goals and drive success in the future.

9

Chapter 9: Lean Metrics and Performance Measurement

Key Lean Metrics: OEE, Cycle Time, Lead Time, etc.

In the bustling analytics center at Aurora Electronics, Sarah Mitchell and James Thompson led a workshop on key lean metrics and performance measurement. Surrounded by computer monitors displaying data dashboards and performance indicators, analysts and managers gathered eagerly, ready to delve into the world of lean metrics.

Sarah began, "Good morning, everyone. Today, we're going to explore key lean metrics and performance measurement techniques essential for assessing and improving our operational efficiency and effectiveness. By understanding these metrics, we can identify areas for improvement and drive continuous progress."

James added, "Key lean metrics provide valuable insights into our processes, performance, and overall productivity. Let's dive in and explore some of the most important metrics used in lean management."

Key Lean Metrics:

Sarah introduced the key lean metrics to the workshop participants, "Key lean metrics are performance indicators that help us assess the health and efficiency of our processes. By measuring these metrics, we can identify opportunities for improvement and monitor our progress over time."

James elaborated, "Some of the key lean metrics include:

1. **Overall Equipment Effectiveness (OEE):** OEE measures the efficiency of equipment and machinery by taking into account availability, performance, and quality. It provides insights into equipment downtime, speed losses, and defects, allowing us to optimize equipment utilization and minimize waste.
2. **Cycle Time:** Cycle time measures the total time required to complete a process or task, from start to finish. It helps us identify bottlenecks, inefficiencies, and opportunities for streamlining our processes to improve productivity and throughput.
3. **Lead Time:** Lead time measures the total time it takes to fulfill a customer order, from the moment it is placed to the moment it is delivered. It provides insights into our responsiveness to customer demand and helps us identify opportunities for reducing delays and improving customer satisfaction.
4. **Takt Time:** Takt time is the rate at which products need to be produced to meet customer demand. It helps us align our production processes with customer requirements and ensures a steady flow of work through our operations.

5. **First-Time Yield (FTY):** FTY measures the percentage of products or services that meet quality standards on the first attempt. It helps us identify defects and errors early in the process, reducing rework and improving overall quality.
6. **Throughput:** Throughput measures the rate at which products or services are produced or delivered within a given time frame. It helps us assess our production capacity and identify opportunities for increasing output without sacrificing quality.
7. **Inventory Turns:** Inventory turns measure the frequency with which inventory is replenished or sold within a given time period. It helps us optimize inventory levels, reduce carrying costs, and improve cash flow."

Interactive Analysis:

Sarah and James facilitated an interactive analysis session where participants analyzed real-world data sets and performance metrics to identify trends, patterns, and areas for improvement. Participants collaborated to interpret the data and develop action plans for driving performance improvements.

Conclusion: Leveraging Lean Metrics

As the workshop concluded, Sarah and James encouraged participants to leverage lean metrics in their daily operations and decision-making processes. "By understanding and measuring key lean metrics, we can identify opportunities for improvement and drive continuous progress toward operational excellence," Sarah said.

James nodded in agreement, "Let's commit ourselves to leveraging lean metrics to optimize our processes, improve our performance, and deliver value to our customers. Together, we can achieve greatness."

The participants left the analytics center feeling empowered and equipped with the knowledge and tools necessary to leverage lean metrics to drive performance improvements. With a renewed focus on measuring and monitoring key performance indicators, Aurora Electronics was well-positioned to achieve its goals of operational excellence and customer satisfaction.

Setting Performance Goals

In the strategy meeting at Aurora Electronics, Sarah Mitchell and James Thompson led a discussion on setting performance goals aligned with key lean metrics. Surrounded by whiteboards displaying charts, graphs, and data analyses, department heads and team leaders gathered eagerly, ready to define objectives and targets for driving continuous improvement.

Sarah began, "Good morning, everyone. Today, we're going to discuss setting performance goals aligned with key lean metrics to drive our organization toward operational excellence. By establishing clear objectives and targets, we can focus our efforts on areas that will have the greatest impact on our performance and productivity."

James added, "Setting performance goals allows us to track our progress, identify areas for improvement, and drive continuous growth. Let's dive in and explore how we can define meaningful goals that align with our key lean metrics."

Setting Performance Goals:
Sarah introduced the process for setting performance goals, "Setting performance goals involves defining specific, mea-

surable, achievable, relevant, and time-bound objectives that align with our key lean metrics. By establishing clear goals, we can create a roadmap for success and ensure alignment across departments and teams."

James elaborated, "Some of the key steps in setting performance goals include:

1. **Identifying Key Metrics:** Start by identifying the key lean metrics that are most relevant to your department or team. These metrics should align with your overall business objectives and reflect areas where improvement is needed.
2. **Analyzing Current Performance:** Analyze your current performance against the key lean metrics to identify strengths, weaknesses, and opportunities for improvement. Use data analysis and benchmarking to understand where you stand relative to industry standards and best practices.
3. **Defining Objectives:** Based on your analysis, define specific objectives and targets for improvement. Ensure that your goals are SMART—specific, measurable, achievable, relevant, and time-bound—to provide clarity and focus.
4. **Aligning with Business Objectives:** Ensure that your performance goals align with the broader business objectives and strategic priorities of the organization. By linking your goals to the overall mission and vision, you can ensure alignment and drive collective progress toward organizational success.
5. **Communicating Goals:** Communicate your performance goals clearly and transparently to all stakeholders,

including employees, managers, and executives. Ensure that everyone understands their role in achieving the goals and the importance of their contribution to the organization's success.
6. **Monitoring Progress:** Continuously monitor progress toward your performance goals using key lean metrics and performance indicators. Regularly review and analyze data to identify trends, patterns, and areas for improvement, and adjust your strategies and tactics accordingly."

Interactive Goal-Setting:

Sarah and James facilitated an interactive goal-setting session where department heads and team leaders worked together to define objectives and targets aligned with key lean metrics. Participants collaborated to set SMART goals and develop action plans for achieving them.

Conclusion: Driving Performance Improvement

As the strategy meeting concluded, Sarah and James encouraged participants to implement the performance goals they had defined and monitor progress closely. "By setting clear and ambitious performance goals aligned with key lean metrics, we can drive continuous improvement and achieve operational excellence," Sarah said.

James nodded in agreement, "Let's commit ourselves to achieving our performance goals and driving positive change across the organization. Together, we can reach new heights of success."

The participants left the strategy meeting feeling motivated and focused, ready to implement their performance goals and drive continuous improvement. With a renewed commitment to setting and achieving meaningful objectives, Aurora Electronics was well-positioned to achieve its goals of operational excellence and customer satisfaction.

Using Metrics to Drive Improvement

In the vibrant workshop space at Aurora Electronics, Sarah Mitchell and James Thompson led a workshop on using metrics to drive improvement. Surrounded by whiteboards filled with charts, graphs, and performance data, employees from various departments gathered eagerly, ready to learn how to leverage metrics to enhance their processes and performance.

Sarah began, "Good afternoon, everyone. Today, we're going to explore how we can use metrics to drive improvement in our processes and performance. By analyzing data, identifying trends, and taking action based on insights, we can achieve greater efficiency, effectiveness, and customer satisfaction."

James added, "Using metrics to drive improvement allows us to make data-driven decisions, prioritize initiatives, and track progress toward our goals. Let's dive in and explore how we can leverage metrics to drive continuous improvement."

Using Metrics to Drive Improvement:

Sarah introduced the process for using metrics to drive improvement, "Using metrics to drive improvement involves a systematic approach to analyzing data, identifying opportunities for optimization, and implementing changes to achieve better outcomes."

James elaborated, "Some of the key steps in using metrics to drive improvement include:

1. **Collecting and Analyzing Data:** Start by collecting relevant data on key performance metrics, such as cycle time, lead time, and quality. Analyze the data to identify trends, patterns, and areas for improvement.
2. **Identifying Opportunities:** Use data analysis to identify opportunities for optimization and efficiency gains. Look for bottlenecks, inefficiencies, and sources of waste that can be addressed to improve performance.
3. **Setting Improvement Targets:** Based on your analysis, set specific improvement targets for key performance metrics. Define measurable objectives that align with your overall business goals and priorities.
4. **Developing Action Plans:** Develop action plans to address the identified opportunities for improvement. Define concrete steps, assign responsibilities, and set timelines for implementation.
5. **Implementing Changes:** Implement the changes outlined in your action plans, leveraging lean principles and best practices to drive continuous improvement. Monitor progress closely and make adjustments as needed.
6. **Monitoring Performance:** Continuously monitor performance against key metrics to track progress toward improvement targets. Use data dashboards, performance reports, and regular reviews to stay informed and identify areas for further optimization."

Interactive Workshop:

Sarah and James facilitated an interactive workshop where employees worked in teams to analyze performance data, identify improvement opportunities, and develop action plans for driving change. Participants collaborated to brainstorm innovative solutions and share best practices for leveraging metrics to drive improvement.

Conclusion: Driving Continuous Improvement

As the workshop concluded, Sarah and James encouraged participants to apply the principles and techniques they had learned to their daily work. "By using metrics to drive improvement, we can achieve greater efficiency, effectiveness, and customer satisfaction," Sarah said.

James nodded in agreement, "Let's commit ourselves to making data-driven decisions, prioritizing initiatives, and driving continuous improvement in everything we do. Together, we can achieve excellence."

The participants left the workshop feeling inspired and empowered, ready to apply their newfound knowledge and skills to drive improvement in their processes and performance. With a renewed focus on using metrics to drive improvement, Aurora Electronics was well-positioned to achieve its goals of operational excellence and customer satisfaction.

Visual Management and Dashboards

In the bustling control room at Aurora Electronics, Sarah Mitchell and James Thompson oversaw the implementation of visual management and dashboards. Surrounded by large monitors displaying real-time data dashboards and performance metrics, operators and managers worked diligently to ensure that the new visual management system was up and running smoothly.

Sarah began, "Good morning, everyone. Today, we're rolling out our new visual management system and dashboards, which will provide us with real-time insights into

CHAPTER 9: LEAN METRICS AND PERFORMANCE MEASUREMENT

our performance and progress toward our goals. By visualizing key metrics and data, we can make better decisions, identify opportunities for improvement, and drive continuous growth."

James added, "Visual management and dashboards enable us to communicate information effectively, engage employees, and foster a culture of transparency and accountability. Let's ensure that our visual management system is implemented successfully and delivers value to our organization."

Implementing Visual Management and Dashboards:

Sarah introduced the process for implementing visual management and dashboards, "Implementing visual management and dashboards involves designing, deploying, and maintaining a system for visualizing key metrics and data in real time."

James elaborated, "Some of the key steps in implementing visual management and dashboards include:

1. **Designing Dashboards:** Start by designing dashboards that visualize key performance metrics and data relevant to your department or team. Ensure that the layout is clear, intuitive, and easy to understand, with visual cues and indicators that highlight important information.
2. **Selecting Visualization Tools:** Choose the right visualization tools and software to create and display your dashboards. Consider factors such as ease of use, compatibility with existing systems, and scalability for future expansion.
3. **Gathering Data:** Gather the necessary data sources and feeds to populate your dashboards with real-time information. Ensure that the data is accurate, reliable,

and up to date, and that it provides a comprehensive view of your performance.
4. **Deploying Dashboards:** Deploy your dashboards across the organization, making them accessible to employees, managers, and executives. Provide training and support to ensure that everyone knows how to use the dashboards effectively and derive value from them.
5. **Monitoring and Maintenance:** Continuously monitor and maintain your dashboards to ensure their accuracy, reliability, and relevance. Regularly review and update the data sources, visualizations, and layouts to reflect changes in your processes and performance.
6. **Driving Engagement:** Use your dashboards to drive engagement and accountability among employees. Encourage teams to use the dashboards to track their progress, identify areas for improvement, and celebrate successes."

Interactive Deployment:

Sarah and James oversaw the deployment of the visual management system, providing guidance and support to operators and managers as they set up and configured the dashboards. Participants worked together to ensure that the dashboards were tailored to their specific needs and preferences, incorporating feedback and suggestions from all stakeholders.

Conclusion: Enhancing Performance Visibility

As the deployment concluded, Sarah and James congratulated the team on a successful implementation. "By implementing visual management and dashboards, we can enhance our performance visibility, make better decisions, and drive continuous improvement," Sarah said.

James nodded in agreement, "Let's commit ourselves to using our new visual management system to its fullest potential, leveraging real-time insights to achieve our goals and deliver value to our customers. Together, we can achieve greatness."

The operators and managers left the control room feeling excited and empowered, ready to use the new visual management system to track their performance, identify opportunities for improvement, and drive continuous growth. With a renewed focus on visual management and dashboards, Aurora Electronics was well-positioned to achieve its goals of operational excellence and customer satisfaction.

Case Studies: Lean Metrics in Action

In the conference room at Aurora Electronics, Sarah Mitchell and James Thompson presented case studies showcasing examples of lean metrics in action. Surrounded by charts, graphs, and data visualizations, managers and executives gathered eagerly, ready to learn from real-world examples of how lean metrics drive improvement and success.

Sarah began, "Good afternoon, everyone. Today, we're going to explore case studies that demonstrate the power of lean metrics in driving improvement, efficiency, and effectiveness in organizations. By examining these examples, we can gain valuable insights into how lean metrics can be used to achieve operational excellence and deliver value to customers."

James added, "Case studies provide us with tangible examples of how organizations have successfully leveraged lean metrics to drive positive change and achieve their goals. Let's dive in and explore these case studies together."

Case Study 1: Toyota

Sarah presented the first case study, "Toyota is a prime example of how lean metrics can drive improvement and innovation in manufacturing. Through its use of key metrics such as OEE, cycle time, and lead time, Toyota has been able to optimize its production processes, reduce waste, and deliver high-quality products to customers."

James elaborated, "By measuring and analyzing key performance metrics in real time, Toyota has been able to identify inefficiencies, bottlenecks, and areas for improvement in its operations. This data-driven approach has enabled Toyota to continuously refine its processes, increase productivity, and maintain its leadership position in the automotive industry."

Case Study 2: Amazon

Sarah introduced the second case study, "Amazon is another example of how lean metrics can drive success in e-commerce. Through its use of metrics such as throughput, first-time yield, and inventory turns, Amazon has been able to optimize its fulfillment processes, reduce delivery times, and improve customer satisfaction."

James explained, "By measuring and monitoring key performance metrics in its fulfillment centers, Amazon can quickly identify issues, such as bottlenecks or inventory shortages, and take corrective action. This proactive approach has enabled Amazon to maintain high levels of efficiency and reliability in its operations, even during periods of peak demand."

Case Study 3: Southwest Airlines

Sarah presented the third case study, "Southwest Airlines demonstrates how lean metrics can drive efficiency and performance in the airline industry. Through its use of metrics such as on-time performance, aircraft utilization, and fuel efficiency, Southwest has been able to optimize its flight schedules, reduce costs, and improve customer satisfaction."

James elaborated, "By closely monitoring key performance metrics in its operations, Southwest can identify opportunities to streamline its processes, improve resource allocation, and enhance overall performance. This data-driven approach has enabled Southwest to maintain its position as one of the most successful and admired airlines in the world."

Conclusion: Learning from Success

As the presentation concluded, Sarah and James encouraged the managers and executives to reflect on the key lessons learned from the case studies. "By studying these examples of lean metrics in action, we can gain valuable insights into how metrics can drive improvement and success in our own organization," Sarah said.

James nodded in agreement, "Let's apply these lessons to our own operations, leveraging lean metrics to drive positive change and achieve our goals. Together, we can achieve greatness."

The managers and executives left the conference room feeling inspired and motivated, ready to apply the lessons learned from the case studies to their own operations and decision-making processes. With a renewed focus on lean metrics, Aurora Electronics was well-positioned to achieve its goals of operational excellence and customer satisfaction.

Adjusting Metrics for Continuous Improvement

In the strategy session at Aurora Electronics, Sarah Mitchell and James Thompson led a discussion on adjusting metrics for continuous improvement. Surrounded by whiteboards filled with charts, graphs, and performance data, department heads and team leaders gathered eagerly, ready to explore how they could refine their metrics to drive even greater efficiency and effectiveness.

Sarah began, "Good morning, everyone. Today, we're going to discuss how we can adjust our metrics for continuous improvement, ensuring that our performance measurement systems evolve along with our processes. By refining our metrics, we can better align them with our goals and priorities, driving continuous progress and success."

James added, "Adjusting metrics for continuous improvement involves a dynamic and iterative process of analysis, feedback, and refinement. Let's dive in and explore how we can adapt our metrics to support our ongoing efforts to achieve operational excellence."

Adjusting Metrics for Continuous Improvement:

Sarah introduced the process for adjusting metrics for continuous improvement, "Adjusting metrics for continuous improvement involves regularly reviewing and refining our performance measurement systems to ensure that they remain relevant, meaningful, and aligned with our goals and priorities."

James elaborated, "Some of the key steps in adjusting metrics for continuous improvement include:

1. **Reviewing Performance Data:** Start by reviewing

performance data and metrics on a regular basis to identify trends, patterns, and areas for improvement. Use data analysis and benchmarking to understand how your performance compares to industry standards and best practices.
2. **Seeking Feedback:** Solicit feedback from stakeholders, including employees, managers, and customers, on the effectiveness and relevance of your metrics. Use their input to identify opportunities for refinement and enhancement.
3. **Identifying Gaps:** Identify any gaps or deficiencies in your current performance measurement systems that may be hindering your ability to achieve your goals. Look for areas where additional or revised metrics may be needed to provide a more comprehensive view of your performance.
4. **Defining New Metrics:** Based on your analysis and feedback, define new metrics or revise existing ones to better align with your goals and priorities. Ensure that your metrics are specific, measurable, achievable, relevant, and time-bound (SMART) to provide clarity and focus.
5. **Implementing Changes:** Implement the changes to your performance measurement systems, including updating dashboards, reports, and data collection processes as necessary. Communicate the changes to all stakeholders to ensure alignment and understanding.
6. **Monitoring Impact:** Continuously monitor the impact of the changes to your metrics on your performance and operations. Assess whether the adjustments have led to improvements in efficiency, effectiveness, and overall

performance.

Interactive Discussion:

Sarah and James facilitated an interactive discussion where department heads and team leaders shared their experiences and insights on adjusting metrics for continuous improvement. Participants exchanged ideas, best practices, and lessons learned, providing valuable input for refining their own performance measurement systems.

Conclusion: Driving Continuous Progress

As the strategy session concluded, Sarah and James encouraged participants to apply the principles and techniques they had discussed to their own operations. "By adjusting our metrics for continuous improvement, we can ensure that our performance measurement systems evolve along with our processes, driving continuous progress and success," Sarah said.

James nodded in agreement, "Let's commit ourselves to regularly reviewing, refining, and adapting our metrics to support our ongoing efforts to achieve operational excellence. Together, we can achieve greatness."

The participants left the strategy session feeling energized and motivated, ready to apply the insights and strategies they had gained to refine their metrics and drive continuous improvement in their operations. With a renewed focus on adjusting metrics for continuous improvement, Aurora Electronics was well-positioned to achieve its goals of operational excellence and customer satisfaction.

10

Chapter 10: Lean in Manufacturing

Lean Manufacturing Principles

In the heart of the Aurora Electronics manufacturing plant, Sarah Mitchell and James Thompson conducted a workshop on lean manufacturing principles. Surrounded by humming machinery and bustling workers, engineers and supervisors gathered eagerly, ready to delve into the fundamental principles that would revolutionize their approach to production.

Sarah began, "Good morning, everyone. Today, we're embarking on a journey into the world of lean manufacturing principles. By understanding and implementing these principles, we can transform our manufacturing processes to achieve greater efficiency, quality, and customer satisfaction."

James added, "Lean manufacturing principles provide us with a framework for streamlining our operations, eliminating waste, and maximizing value for our customers. Let's explore these principles together and discover how they can revolutionize our approach to manufacturing."

Lean Manufacturing Principles:

Sarah introduced the core principles of lean manufacturing, "At its core, lean manufacturing is about maximizing customer value while minimizing waste. It is based on a set of principles and practices that aim to create a smooth, efficient, and responsive production system."

James elaborated, "Some of the key principles of lean manufacturing include:

1. **Identifying Value:** The first step in lean manufacturing is to identify the value that customers are willing to pay for. This value is defined by the features, functions, and quality of the product or service.
2. **Mapping the Value Stream:** Once value is identified, the next step is to map the value stream—the series of steps required to deliver the product or service to the customer. This involves identifying all the activities, processes, and resources involved in creating and delivering value.
3. **Creating Flow:** Lean manufacturing aims to create a continuous flow of work through the value stream, with minimal interruptions, delays, and waste. This requires streamlining processes, reducing batch sizes, and synchronizing activities to eliminate bottlenecks and inefficiencies.
4. **Pull Production:** In lean manufacturing, production is driven by customer demand, rather than by forecasts or schedules. This is achieved through a pull system, where work is pulled through the value stream based on customer orders or consumption.

5. **Striving for Perfection:** Lean manufacturing is a journey of continuous improvement, with the goal of achieving perfection—delivering the highest quality products and services, at the lowest cost, with the shortest lead times. This requires a culture of continuous learning, experimentation, and innovation."

Interactive Workshop:

Sarah and James facilitated an interactive workshop where participants explored each lean manufacturing principle in depth. Through group discussions, case studies, and hands-on exercises, participants gained a deeper understanding of how these principles could be applied to their own manufacturing processes.

Conclusion: Embracing Lean Manufacturing

As the workshop concluded, Sarah and James encouraged participants to embrace lean manufacturing principles in their daily work. "By implementing lean manufacturing principles, we can transform our manufacturing processes to achieve greater efficiency, quality, and customer satisfaction," Sarah said.

James nodded in agreement, "Let's commit ourselves to embracing lean manufacturing principles and driving continuous improvement in our operations. Together, we can achieve excellence in manufacturing."

The participants left the workshop feeling inspired and motivated, ready to apply the principles they had learned to revolutionize their approach to manufacturing. With a renewed focus on lean manufacturing, Aurora Electronics was well-positioned to achieve its goals of operational excellence and customer satisfaction.

Lean Techniques for Manufacturing

In the bustling factory floor of Aurora Electronics, Sarah Mitchell and James Thompson led a training session on lean techniques for manufacturing. Surrounded by assembly lines and production equipment, operators and technicians gathered eagerly, ready to learn how they could apply lean techniques to optimize their work processes.

Sarah began, "Good afternoon, everyone. Today, we're going to explore a variety of lean techniques that can help us streamline our manufacturing processes, eliminate waste, and improve overall efficiency. By mastering these techniques, we can enhance our productivity and deliver greater value to our customers."

James added, "Lean techniques provide us with practical tools and methods for identifying and addressing inefficiencies in our operations. Let's dive in and discover how these techniques can revolutionize the way we work."

Lean Techniques for Manufacturing:

Sarah introduced the key lean techniques for manufacturing, "Lean techniques encompass a wide range of tools and methods that can be applied to various aspects of the manufacturing process. These techniques are designed to identify and eliminate waste, improve flow, and enhance overall performance."

James elaborated, "Some of the most commonly used lean techniques for manufacturing include:

1. **5S:** 5S is a systematic approach to workplace organization that involves sorting, setting in order, shining, standardizing, and sustaining. By organizing the workspace

and eliminating clutter, 5S creates a clean, efficient, and safe environment for work.
2. **Kaizen:** Kaizen, or continuous improvement, is the practice of making small, incremental changes to processes and systems to achieve better results over time. By encouraging employees to identify and implement improvements on a daily basis, Kaizen drives continuous growth and innovation.
3. **Poka-Yoke:** Poka-Yoke, or mistake-proofing, involves designing processes and systems in a way that prevents errors and defects from occurring. By implementing mechanisms such as sensors, alarms, and visual cues, Poka-Yoke minimizes the risk of mistakes and improves quality.
4. **SMED:** SMED, or Single-Minute Exchange of Dies, is a technique for reducing setup times and changeover times in manufacturing processes. By streamlining the setup and changeover procedures, SMED enables faster, more efficient production runs and reduces downtime.
5. **Kanban:** Kanban is a visual scheduling system that uses cards or signals to control the flow of work through the production process. By visualizing workflow, limiting work in progress, and balancing demand with capacity, Kanban helps to optimize production and minimize waste.
6. **Total Productive Maintenance (TPM):** TPM is a proactive approach to equipment maintenance that aims to maximize equipment uptime and reliability. By involving operators in maintenance activities and implementing preventive and predictive maintenance practices, TPM ensures that equipment operates at peak performance

levels.

Interactive Training Session:

Sarah and James led an interactive training session where operators and technicians had the opportunity to learn and practice each lean technique. Through hands-on exercises, simulations, and real-world examples, participants gained valuable insights into how they could apply these techniques to their own work processes.

Conclusion: Driving Efficiency and Excellence

As the training session concluded, Sarah and James encouraged participants to begin implementing the lean techniques they had learned. "By mastering these lean techniques, we can drive efficiency, productivity, and excellence in our manufacturing processes," Sarah said.

James nodded in agreement, "Let's commit ourselves to applying these techniques consistently and continuously improving our operations. Together, we can achieve greatness in manufacturing."

The operators and technicians left the training session feeling empowered and motivated, ready to apply the lean techniques they had learned to optimize their work processes and drive continuous improvement. With a renewed focus on lean manufacturing, Aurora Electronics was well-positioned to achieve its goals of operational excellence and customer satisfaction.

Case Studies: Lean Manufacturing Success

In the conference room at Aurora Electronics, Sarah Mitchell and James Thompson presented case studies showcasing examples of lean manufacturing success. Surrounded by charts, graphs, and data visualizations, managers and executives gathered eagerly, ready to gain insights from real-world examples of how lean manufacturing principles and techniques had transformed organizations.

Sarah began, "Good morning, everyone. Today, we're going to explore case studies that demonstrate the power of lean manufacturing to drive success and excellence in organizations. By studying these examples, we can gain valuable insights into how lean principles and techniques can be applied to achieve operational excellence and deliver value to customers."

James added, "Case studies provide us with tangible examples of how organizations have successfully implemented lean manufacturing principles and techniques to improve efficiency, quality, and customer satisfaction. Let's dive in and explore these case studies together."

Case Study 1: Toyota

Sarah presented the first case study, "Toyota is widely recognized as a pioneer of lean manufacturing, with its Toyota Production System (TPS) serving as a model for organizations around the world. Through its relentless focus on eliminating waste, improving flow, and empowering employees, Toyota has achieved unparalleled levels of efficiency, quality, and customer satisfaction."

James elaborated, "By implementing lean manufacturing principles such as Just-In-Time (JIT) production, Kanban systems, and Total Productive Maintenance (TPM), Toyota has been able to optimize its operations and drive continuous improvement. This commitment to lean principles has enabled Toyota to maintain its position as one of the most successful and admired automakers in the world."

Case Study 2: Boeing

Sarah introduced the second case study, "Boeing is another example of how lean manufacturing can drive success in the aerospace industry. Through its use of lean techniques such as value stream mapping, SMED, and Kaizen events, Boeing has been able to streamline its production processes, reduce lead times, and improve quality."

James explained, "By engaging employees in continuous improvement initiatives and empowering them to identify and implement changes, Boeing has been able to achieve significant improvements in efficiency and productivity. This focus on lean manufacturing has enabled Boeing to maintain its position as a global leader in aerospace innovation and technology."

Case Study 3: Tesla

Sarah presented the third case study, "Tesla is a prime example of how lean manufacturing principles can drive success in the electric vehicle industry. Through its use of advanced robotics, digital manufacturing technologies, and lean techniques such as 5S and Poka-Yoke, Tesla has been able to revolutionize automotive production."

James elaborated, "By adopting lean principles and practices from the outset, Tesla has been able to design and manufacture vehicles with unprecedented speed, efficiency, and quality. This commitment to lean manufacturing has enabled Tesla to disrupt the automotive industry and accelerate the transition to sustainable transportation."

Conclusion: Learning from Success

As the presentation concluded, Sarah and James encouraged the managers and executives to reflect on the key lessons learned from the case studies. "By studying these examples of lean manufacturing success, we can gain valuable insights into how lean principles and techniques can drive improvement and innovation in our own organization," Sarah said.

James nodded in agreement, "Let's apply these lessons to our own operations, leveraging lean principles and techniques to achieve operational excellence and deliver value to our customers. Together, we can achieve greatness."

The managers and executives left the conference room feeling inspired and motivated, ready to apply the lessons learned from the case studies to their own operations and decision-making processes. With a renewed focus on lean manufacturing, Aurora Electronics was well-positioned to achieve its goals of operational excellence and customer satisfaction.

Overcoming Challenges in Lean Manufacturing

In the strategy session at Aurora Electronics, Sarah Mitchell and James Thompson led a discussion on overcoming challenges in lean manufacturing. Surrounded by whiteboards filled with diagrams and data, engineers and managers gathered eagerly, ready to tackle the obstacles that stood in the way of implementing lean principles and techniques.

Sarah began, "Good afternoon, everyone. Today, we're going to explore the challenges that organizations often face when implementing lean manufacturing principles and techniques. By identifying and addressing these challenges, we can ensure a smoother and more successful transition to lean manufacturing."

James added, "While lean manufacturing offers numerous benefits, it also presents its own set of challenges. Let's dive in and discuss how we can overcome these challenges and achieve success in our lean journey."

Overcoming Challenges in Lean Manufacturing:

Sarah introduced the key challenges in lean manufacturing and strategies for overcoming them, "Implementing lean manufacturing principles and techniques can be a complex and challenging process. Some of the common challenges include resistance to change, lack of employee engagement, and difficulty sustaining improvements over time."

James elaborated, "To overcome these challenges, organizations need to focus on several key strategies:

1. **Leadership Commitment:** Leadership commitment is essential for the success of lean initiatives. Leaders need to champion lean principles, set clear goals and expectations, and provide the necessary resources and support for implementation.
2. **Employee Engagement:** Engaging employees in the lean process is critical for success. Organizations should involve employees in problem-solving, decision-making, and continuous improvement initiatives, empowering them to take ownership of the lean journey.
3. **Training and Education:** Providing training and education on lean principles and techniques is essential for building knowledge and skills among employees. Organizations should invest in comprehensive training

programs to ensure that employees understand lean concepts and methodologies.
4. **Continuous Improvement:** Lean manufacturing is a journey of continuous improvement. Organizations should establish systems and processes for monitoring performance, identifying opportunities for improvement, and implementing changes on an ongoing basis.
5. **Culture of Excellence:** Creating a culture of excellence is key to sustaining lean initiatives over the long term. Organizations should foster a culture of accountability, collaboration, and innovation, where employees are empowered to strive for excellence in everything they do."

Interactive Discussion:

Sarah and James facilitated an interactive discussion where engineers and managers shared their experiences and insights on overcoming challenges in lean manufacturing. Participants exchanged ideas, best practices, and lessons learned, providing valuable input for addressing challenges in their own lean journey.

Conclusion: Achieving Success in Lean Manufacturing

As the strategy session concluded, Sarah and James encouraged participants to apply the strategies discussed to overcome challenges in their own lean journey. "By addressing these challenges head-on and staying committed to our lean principles, we can achieve success in our manufacturing operations," Sarah said.

James nodded in agreement, "Let's work together to overcome obstacles, drive continuous improvement, and achieve excellence in manufacturing. Together, we can achieve greatness."

The engineers and managers left the strategy session feeling inspired and motivated, ready to apply the strategies they had learned to overcome challenges and drive success in their lean journey. With a renewed focus on addressing challenges in lean manufacturing, Aurora Electronics was well-positioned to achieve its goals of operational excellence and customer satisfaction.

Lean Manufacturing Tools

In the workshop at Aurora Electronics, Sarah Mitchell and James Thompson introduced the team to various lean manufacturing tools. Surrounded by workstations and prototypes, engineers and technicians gathered eagerly, ready to explore the tools that would help them optimize their manufacturing processes.

Sarah began, "Good morning, everyone. Today, we're going to delve into the world of lean manufacturing tools—practical techniques and methods that can help us streamline our operations, eliminate waste, and improve efficiency. By mastering these tools, we can achieve excellence in manufacturing."

James added, "Lean manufacturing tools provide us with a structured approach to identifying and addressing inefficiencies in our processes. Let's dive in and discover how these tools can revolutionize the way we work."

Lean Manufacturing Tools:

Sarah introduced the key lean manufacturing tools and their applications, "Lean manufacturing tools encompass a wide range of techniques and methods that can be applied to various aspects of the manufacturing process. These tools

CHAPTER 10: LEAN IN MANUFACTURING

are designed to help us identify and eliminate waste, improve flow, and enhance overall performance."

James elaborated, "Some of the most commonly used lean manufacturing tools include:

1. **Value Stream Mapping:** Value Stream Mapping is a visual tool used to analyze and map the flow of materials and information through the production process. By identifying value-added and non-value-added activities, Value Stream Mapping helps us pinpoint areas for improvement and streamline our operations.
2. **5S:** 5S is a systematic approach to workplace organization that involves sorting, setting in order, shining, standardizing, and sustaining. By organizing the workspace and eliminating clutter, 5S creates a clean, efficient, and safe environment for work.
3. **Kaizen Events:** Kaizen Events are focused, short-term improvement projects aimed at addressing specific issues or opportunities in the production process. By bringing together cross-functional teams to collaborate on problem-solving, Kaizen Events drive rapid improvements in efficiency and quality.
4. **Kanban System:** The Kanban System is a visual scheduling system that uses cards or signals to control the flow of work through the production process. By visualizing workflow, limiting work in progress, and balancing demand with capacity, Kanban helps us optimize production and minimize waste.
5. **Poka-Yoke (Error Proofing):** Poka-Yoke involves designing processes and systems in a way that prevents errors and defects from occurring. By implementing

mechanisms such as sensors, alarms, and visual cues, Poka-Yoke minimizes the risk of mistakes and improves quality.
6. **SMED (Single-Minute Exchange of Dies):** SMED is a technique for reducing setup times and changeover times in manufacturing processes. By streamlining the setup and changeover procedures, SMED enables faster, more efficient production runs and reduces downtime."

Interactive Workshop:

Sarah and James led an interactive workshop where engineers and technicians had the opportunity to learn and practice each lean manufacturing tool. Through hands-on exercises, simulations, and real-world examples, participants gained valuable insights into how they could apply these tools to optimize their work processes.

Conclusion: Empowering Excellence in Manufacturing

As the workshop concluded, Sarah and James encouraged participants to begin applying the lean manufacturing tools they had learned. "By mastering these tools, we can drive efficiency, productivity, and excellence in our manufacturing processes," Sarah said.

James nodded in agreement, "Let's commit ourselves to applying these tools consistently and continuously improving our operations. Together, we can achieve greatness in manufacturing."

The engineers and technicians left the workshop feeling empowered and motivated, ready to apply the lean manufacturing tools they had learned to optimize their work processes and drive continuous improvement. With a renewed focus on lean manufacturing, Aurora Electronics was well-positioned to achieve its goals of operational excellence and customer satisfaction.

Future Trends in Lean Manufacturing

In the innovation lab at Aurora Electronics, Sarah Mitchell and James Thompson led a discussion on future trends in lean manufacturing. Surrounded by prototypes, advanced machinery, and cutting-edge technology, engineers and researchers gathered eagerly, ready to explore the emerging trends that would shape the future of manufacturing.

Sarah began, "Good afternoon, everyone. Today, we're going to look ahead and explore the future of lean manufacturing—emerging trends, technologies, and innovations that will revolutionize the way we produce and deliver products. By staying ahead of the curve, we can position ourselves for success in the ever-evolving world of manufacturing."

James added, "As technology advances and customer expectations evolve, lean manufacturing will continue to adapt and evolve. Let's dive in and discover the future trends that will shape the next generation of manufacturing."

Future Trends in Lean Manufacturing:
Sarah introduced the key future trends in lean manufacturing and their potential impact, "The future of lean manufacturing is marked by rapid technological advancements, digital transformation, and a shift towards sustainability and flexibility. Some of the emerging trends that we need to watch out for include:

1. **Digitalization and Industry 4.0:** The integration of digital technologies such as artificial intelligence, Internet of Things (IoT), and data analytics will revolutionize manufacturing processes. Industry 4.0 initiatives will enable real-time monitoring, predictive maintenance, and smart decision-making, leading to greater efficiency and agility.
2. **Additive Manufacturing (3D Printing):** Additive manufacturing technologies such as 3D printing will enable on-demand production, customization, and rapid prototyping. By reducing lead times, minimizing waste, and enabling decentralized production, additive manufacturing will transform the way we manufacture and distribute products.
3. **Lean Supply Chains:** Lean principles will extend beyond the factory floor to encompass the entire supply chain. Organizations will collaborate closely with suppliers and partners to optimize logistics, reduce inventory, and improve responsiveness to customer demand.
4. **Sustainability and Circular Economy:** There will be a growing emphasis on sustainability and environmental stewardship in manufacturing. Lean principles will be applied to minimize waste, conserve resources, and design products for reuse and recycling, leading to a more sustainable and circular economy.
5. **Human-Machine Collaboration:** Advances in robotics and automation will enable greater collaboration between humans and machines in manufacturing. Augmented reality, wearable devices, and collaborative robots (cobots) will enhance productivity, safety, and ergonomics in the workplace.

6. **Agile Manufacturing:** Lean organizations will embrace agility and flexibility to respond rapidly to changing market conditions and customer preferences. Agile manufacturing practices such as modular production, flexible work cells, and dynamic scheduling will enable organizations to adapt quickly and efficiently to new challenges and opportunities."

Interactive Discussion:

Sarah and James facilitated an interactive discussion where engineers and researchers shared their insights and predictions on future trends in lean manufacturing. Participants exchanged ideas, debated the potential impact of emerging technologies, and brainstormed innovative solutions for the future.

Conclusion: Embracing the Future

As the discussion concluded, Sarah and James encouraged participants to embrace the future of lean manufacturing and stay ahead of the curve. "By anticipating and adapting to emerging trends, we can position ourselves as leaders in the evolving world of manufacturing," Sarah said.

James nodded in agreement, "Let's commit ourselves to innovation, collaboration, and continuous improvement as we navigate the exciting opportunities and challenges that lie ahead. Together, we can shape the future of manufacturing."

The engineers and researchers left the innovation lab feeling inspired and energized, ready to embrace the future of lean manufacturing and drive innovation in their work. With a forward-thinking approach, Aurora Electronics was well-positioned to thrive in the dynamic and ever-changing landscape of manufacturing.

11

Chapter 11: Lean in Service Industries

Applying Lean Principles to Services

In the conference room at Aurora Services headquarters, Sarah Mitchell and James Thompson led a seminar on applying lean principles to services. Surrounded by charts, diagrams, and customer feedback data, service managers and representatives gathered eagerly, ready to explore how lean principles could transform their service delivery processes.

Sarah began, "Good morning, everyone. Today, we're going to delve into the world of lean principles and how they can be applied to service industries. While lean manufacturing has been widely adopted in production settings, lean principles are equally relevant and powerful in service environments. By applying lean principles to our services, we can streamline processes, eliminate waste, and deliver greater value to our customers."

James added, "Service industries, such as healthcare, hospitality, and banking, can benefit immensely from the application of lean principles. Let's dive in and discover how we can leverage lean principles to optimize our service delivery processes and enhance customer satisfaction."

Applying Lean Principles to Services:

Sarah introduced the key concepts of lean principles in services and their applications, "In service industries, lean principles focus on identifying and eliminating waste, improving flow, and enhancing overall efficiency and quality. While the specific challenges and opportunities may vary across different service sectors, the underlying principles remain the same."

James elaborated, "Some of the key ways in which lean principles can be applied to services include:

1. **Value Stream Mapping:** Just as in manufacturing, value stream mapping is a powerful tool for visualizing and analyzing the flow of work in service processes. By identifying value-added and non-value-added activities, service organizations can streamline processes, reduce lead times, and improve customer satisfaction.

2. **Customer Focus:** Lean principles emphasize the importance of understanding and meeting customer needs and expectations. Service organizations should strive to design processes and services from the customer's perspective, minimizing complexity, and maximizing value.

3. **Standardized Work:** Standardized work involves documenting and following standardized procedures and protocols for delivering services. By establishing clear

guidelines and best practices, service organizations can ensure consistency, quality, and efficiency in service delivery.
4. **Continuous Improvement:** Lean is a journey of continuous improvement, and service organizations should embrace a culture of continuous learning and innovation. By empowering employees to identify and implement improvements in service processes, organizations can drive continuous improvement and enhance customer satisfaction.
5. **Employee Engagement:** Engaging employees in the lean process is essential for success in service industries. Service organizations should involve frontline employees in problem-solving, decision-making, and process improvement initiatives, empowering them to contribute to the organization's success.
6. **Measurement and Metrics:** Lean organizations in service industries should establish key performance indicators (KPIs) and metrics to monitor performance, track progress, and identify opportunities for improvement. By measuring and analyzing performance data, organizations can make informed decisions and drive continuous improvement."

Interactive Seminar:

Sarah and James led an interactive seminar where service managers and representatives had the opportunity to discuss and explore the application of lean principles to their specific service processes. Through case studies, group discussions, and brainstorming sessions, participants gained valuable insights into how they could leverage lean principles to optimize service delivery and improve customer satisfaction.

Conclusion: Transforming Service Delivery

As the seminar concluded, Sarah and James encouraged participants to begin applying the lean principles they had learned to their service processes. "By embracing lean principles and driving continuous improvement, we can transform our service delivery processes and deliver greater value to our customers," Sarah said.

James nodded in agreement, "Let's commit ourselves to applying lean principles to our services, driving efficiency, quality, and customer satisfaction. Together, we can achieve excellence in service delivery."

The service managers and representatives left the seminar feeling inspired and motivated, ready to apply the lean principles they had learned to optimize their service delivery processes and drive continuous improvement. With a renewed focus on lean principles, Aurora Services was well-positioned to achieve its goals of customer satisfaction and operational excellence.

Case Studies: Lean in Service Sectors

In the conference room at Aurora Services headquarters, Sarah Mitchell and James Thompson presented case studies showcasing examples of lean principles in action within service sectors. Surrounded by charts, graphs, and customer testimonials, service managers and representatives gathered eagerly, ready to gain insights from real-world examples of how lean principles had transformed service delivery.

Sarah began, "Good morning, everyone. Today, we're going to explore case studies that demonstrate the power of lean principles to drive success and excellence in service sectors. From healthcare to hospitality to financial services, organizations across various industries have successfully applied lean principles to optimize their service delivery processes and enhance customer satisfaction."

James added, "By studying these examples, we can gain valuable insights into how lean principles can be adapted and applied to different service environments. Let's dive in and explore these case studies together."

Case Study 1: Virginia Mason Medical Center

Sarah presented the first case study, "Virginia Mason Medical Center is a prime example of how lean principles can revolutionize healthcare delivery. By adopting lean methodologies such as value stream mapping, standardized work, and continuous improvement, Virginia Mason transformed its operations and achieved significant improvements in patient safety, quality, and efficiency."

James elaborated, "Through its commitment to lean principles, Virginia Mason reduced patient wait times, eliminated waste in administrative processes, and improved the overall patient experience. This focus on continuous improvement has enabled Virginia Mason to maintain its position as a leader in healthcare innovation and patient-centered care."

Case Study 2: Ritz-Carlton Hotel Company

Sarah introduced the second case study, "The Ritz-Carlton Hotel Company is renowned for its commitment to excellence in hospitality. By embracing lean principles such as customer focus, employee engagement, and standardized work, Ritz-Carlton has consistently delivered exceptional service experiences to its guests."

James explained, "Through its relentless pursuit of perfection and dedication to exceeding customer expectations, Ritz-Carlton has earned a reputation for unparalleled luxury and hospitality. This customer-centric approach, rooted in lean principles, has enabled Ritz-Carlton to maintain its position as a global leader in the hospitality industry."

Case Study 3: USAA

Sarah presented the third case study, "USAA is a leading provider of financial services to military members and their families. By applying lean principles such as value stream mapping, continuous improvement, and employee empowerment, USAA has streamlined its processes, improved efficiency, and enhanced customer satisfaction."

James elaborated, "Through its focus on lean principles, USAA has been able to deliver faster, more responsive service to its members, while also reducing costs and improving quality. This commitment to excellence has made USAA a trusted partner for military families seeking financial security and peace of mind."

Conclusion: Learning from Lean Success

As the presentation concluded, Sarah and James encouraged the service managers and representatives to reflect on the key lessons learned from the case studies. "By studying these examples of lean success in service sectors, we can gain valuable insights into how lean principles can drive improvement and innovation in our own organizations," Sarah said.

James nodded in agreement, "Let's apply these lessons to our own service delivery processes, leveraging lean principles to achieve operational excellence and deliver greater value to our customers. Together, we can achieve greatness in service."

The service managers and representatives left the conference room feeling inspired and motivated, ready to apply the lessons learned from the case studies to their own service delivery processes and drive continuous improvement. With a renewed focus on lean principles, Aurora Services was well-positioned to achieve its goals of customer satisfaction and operational excellence.

Lean Tools for Service Improvement

In the training room at Aurora Services headquarters, Sarah Mitchell and James Thompson led a workshop on lean tools for service improvement. Surrounded by whiteboards filled with diagrams and process maps, service managers and representatives gathered eagerly, ready to learn how they could leverage lean tools to optimize their service delivery processes.

Sarah began, "Good morning, everyone. Today, we're going to explore the various lean tools that can be applied to service industries to drive improvement and enhance customer satisfaction. From value stream mapping to standardized work, these tools provide a structured approach to identifying and eliminating waste in service processes."

James added, "By mastering these tools, we can streamline our service delivery processes, improve efficiency, and deliver greater value to our customers. Let's dive in and discover how we can leverage lean tools to achieve service excellence."

Lean Tools for Service Improvement:

Sarah introduced the key lean tools for service improvement and their applications, "Lean tools provide service organizations with practical techniques and methods for identifying and addressing inefficiencies in service delivery processes.

Some of the key lean tools that can be applied to service industries include:

1. **Value Stream Mapping:** Value Stream Mapping is a visual tool used to analyze and map the flow of work in service processes. By identifying value-added and non-value-added activities, service organizations can pinpoint areas for improvement and streamline their processes to deliver greater value to customers.
2. **Standardized Work:** Standardized Work involves documenting and following standardized procedures and protocols for delivering services. By establishing clear guidelines and best practices, service organizations can ensure consistency, quality, and efficiency in service delivery.
3. **Kaizen Events:** Kaizen Events are focused, short-term improvement projects aimed at addressing specific issues or opportunities in service processes. By bringing together cross-functional teams to collaborate on problem-solving, Kaizen Events drive rapid improvements in service delivery.
4. **Customer Journey Mapping:** Customer Journey Mapping is a technique used to visualize and understand the customer's experience with a service from beginning to end. By mapping out the customer's interactions and touchpoints, service organizations can identify pain points and opportunities for improvement in the customer experience.
5. **Gemba Walks:** Gemba Walks involve going to the 'gemba' or the place where the work is done to observe and understand the service delivery process firsthand.

By engaging with frontline employees and customers, service managers can gain valuable insights into how services are delivered and identify opportunities for improvement.
6. **Root Cause Analysis:** Root Cause Analysis is a problem-solving technique used to identify the underlying causes of service issues or problems. By digging deep into the root causes of problems, service organizations can implement effective solutions to prevent them from recurring in the future."

Interactive Workshop:

Sarah and James led an interactive workshop where service managers and representatives had the opportunity to learn and practice each lean tool. Through hands-on exercises, simulations, and real-world examples, participants gained valuable insights into how they could apply these tools to optimize their service delivery processes and drive continuous improvement.

Conclusion: Driving Service Excellence

As the workshop concluded, Sarah and James encouraged participants to begin applying the lean tools they had learned to their service processes. "By mastering these tools and driving continuous improvement, we can achieve excellence in service delivery and deliver greater value to our customers," Sarah said.

James nodded in agreement, "Let's commit ourselves to applying these tools consistently and continuously improving our service delivery processes. Together, we can achieve greatness in service."

The service managers and representatives left the workshop

feeling empowered and motivated, ready to apply the lean tools they had learned to optimize their service delivery processes and drive continuous improvement. With a renewed focus on lean principles, Aurora Services was well-positioned to achieve its goals of customer satisfaction and operational excellence.

Challenges and Solutions in Lean Services

In the strategy room at Aurora Services headquarters, Sarah Mitchell and James Thompson facilitated a discussion on the challenges and solutions in implementing lean principles in service industries. Surrounded by charts displaying process metrics and improvement initiatives, service managers and representatives gathered eagerly, ready to address the obstacles they faced in their lean journey.

Sarah began, "Good morning, everyone. Today, we're going to explore the challenges that service organizations may encounter when implementing lean principles and discuss strategies for overcoming these challenges. While lean principles offer numerous benefits, navigating the complexities of service delivery can present unique challenges that require innovative solutions."

James added, "By identifying and addressing these challenges proactively, we can ensure the success of our lean initiatives and drive continuous improvement in service delivery. Let's dive in and explore the challenges and solutions in lean services together."

Challenges in Lean Services:

Sarah outlined the key challenges in implementing lean principles in service industries, "Some of the challenges that service organizations may face when adopting lean principles include:

1. **Resistance to Change:** Implementing lean principles often requires changes to established processes and ways of working, which can be met with resistance from employees who are comfortable with the status quo.
2. **Complexity of Service Processes:** Service delivery processes are often complex and multifaceted, involving numerous touchpoints and interactions with customers, which can make it challenging to identify and eliminate waste.
3. **Lack of Standardization:** Unlike manufacturing processes, service processes may lack standardized procedures and protocols, making it difficult to achieve consistency and efficiency in service delivery.
4. **Intangible Nature of Services:** Services are often intangible and subjective, making it challenging to measure and quantify improvements in service quality and customer satisfaction.
5. **Customer Expectations:** Customers' expectations for service quality and responsiveness are constantly evolving, requiring service organizations to adapt quickly and continuously improve their processes.
6. **Employee Engagement:** Engaging frontline employees in the lean process and empowering them to drive improvement can be challenging, especially in organizations with hierarchical or rigid structures."

Solutions in Lean Services:

James presented solutions to address these challenges and

drive success in lean services, "While implementing lean principles in service industries may pose challenges, there are several strategies that service organizations can employ to overcome these obstacles:

1. **Leadership Commitment:** Leadership commitment is essential for the success of lean initiatives. Senior leaders should champion the lean journey, communicate the vision for change, and provide the necessary resources and support to empower employees to drive improvement.
2. **Employee Involvement:** Engaging frontline employees in the lean process is critical for success. Service organizations should create opportunities for employees to participate in problem-solving, decision-making, and process improvement initiatives, fostering a culture of ownership and continuous improvement.
3. **Training and Education:** Providing training and education on lean principles and tools is essential for building the capabilities and skills needed to drive improvement in service delivery processes. Service organizations should invest in training programs and workshops to ensure that employees are equipped with the knowledge and skills to succeed.
4. **Standardization and Documentation:** Establishing standardized procedures and protocols for delivering services is key to achieving consistency and efficiency. Service organizations should document best practices and guidelines for service delivery, ensuring that employees have clear expectations and guidelines to follow.
5. **Customer Feedback and Engagement:** Soliciting feedback from customers and involving them in the improve-

ment process is essential for understanding their needs and expectations. Service organizations should actively seek customer input, incorporate feedback into their improvement efforts, and communicate changes and improvements to customers transparently.

6. **Continuous Learning and Adaptation:** Lean is a journey of continuous improvement, and service organizations should embrace a culture of learning and adaptation. Service organizations should regularly review and reflect on their processes, identify opportunities for improvement, and adapt quickly to changes in customer needs and market conditions."

Interactive Discussion:

Sarah and James facilitated an interactive discussion where service managers and representatives shared their experiences and insights on overcoming challenges in lean services. Participants exchanged ideas, shared best practices, and brainstormed innovative solutions to common challenges faced in service industries.

Conclusion: Overcoming Challenges, Driving Success

As the discussion concluded, Sarah and James encouraged the service managers and representatives to apply the strategies and solutions discussed to their own lean initiatives. "By addressing these challenges proactively and leveraging innovative solutions, we can overcome obstacles and drive success in lean services," Sarah said.

James nodded in agreement, "Let's commit ourselves to overcoming challenges and driving continuous improvement in service delivery. Together, we can achieve excellence and deliver greater value to our customers."

The service managers and representatives left the strategy room feeling inspired and empowered, ready to implement the strategies and solutions discussed to overcome challenges and drive success in their lean initiatives. With a renewed focus on addressing challenges proactively, Aurora Services was well-positioned to achieve its goals of customer satisfaction and operational excellence.

Measuring Success in Lean Services

In the boardroom at Aurora Services headquarters, Sarah Mitchell and James Thompson led a meeting to discuss how to measure success in lean services. Surrounded by charts displaying key performance indicators and improvement metrics, service managers and representatives gathered eagerly, ready to learn how they could evaluate the impact of their lean initiatives on service delivery.

Sarah began, "Good morning, everyone. Today, we're going to explore how we can measure success in our lean services initiatives. While implementing lean principles can drive improvements in service delivery processes, it's essential to have metrics and indicators in place to track our progress and evaluate the effectiveness of our efforts."

James added, "By establishing clear performance metrics and measuring our success against them, we can identify areas for improvement, celebrate achievements, and drive continuous improvement in service delivery. Let's dive in and discuss how we can measure success in lean services."

Measuring Success in Lean Services:

Sarah introduced the key metrics and indicators for measuring success in lean services, "Success in lean services can be measured across several dimensions, including:

1. **Service Quality:** Service quality metrics, such as customer satisfaction scores, net promoter scores (NPS), and service level agreements (SLAs), provide insights into the overall quality of service delivery and customer experience.
2. **Efficiency:** Efficiency metrics, such as cycle time, lead time, and throughput, measure the speed and effectiveness of service delivery processes. By reducing cycle times and lead times, service organizations can improve efficiency and responsiveness to customer needs.
3. **Cost Savings:** Cost savings metrics, such as cost per transaction and cost per service, quantify the financial benefits of lean initiatives. By eliminating waste and improving efficiency, service organizations can reduce costs and increase profitability.
4. **Employee Engagement:** Employee engagement metrics, such as employee satisfaction scores and employee turnover rates, gauge the level of employee engagement and satisfaction with lean initiatives. Engaged employees are more likely to contribute to the success of lean initiatives and drive continuous improvement.
5. **Process Improvement:** Process improvement metrics, such as the number of kaizen events conducted and the percentage of process improvements implemented, measure the effectiveness of lean initiatives in driving continuous improvement in service delivery processes.
6. **Business Impact:** Business impact metrics, such as revenue growth, market share, and customer retention rates, assess the overall impact of lean initiatives on the

organization's bottom line and competitive position."

Interactive Discussion:

Sarah and James facilitated an interactive discussion where service managers and representatives shared their perspectives on measuring success in lean services. Participants exchanged ideas, discussed best practices, and identified key metrics relevant to their service delivery processes.

Conclusion: Driving Continuous Improvement

As the meeting concluded, Sarah and James encouraged the service managers and representatives to establish clear performance metrics and track their progress against them. "By measuring our success in lean services and identifying areas for improvement, we can drive continuous improvement and deliver greater value to our customers," Sarah said.

James nodded in agreement, "Let's commit ourselves to tracking our progress, celebrating achievements, and driving continuous improvement in service delivery. Together, we can achieve excellence and deliver exceptional service to our customers."

The service managers and representatives left the boardroom feeling motivated and empowered, ready to establish clear performance metrics and measure success in their lean services initiatives. With a renewed focus on continuous improvement, Aurora Services was well-positioned to achieve its goals of customer satisfaction and operational excellence.

Lean Service Excellence

In the auditorium at Aurora Services headquarters, Sarah Mitchell and James Thompson hosted a special event to celebrate lean service excellence. Service managers, representatives, and frontline employees gathered eagerly, filled with anticipation for the announcement of the winners of the Lean Service Excellence Awards.

Sarah took the stage, the spotlight illuminating her as she addressed the audience, "Good evening, everyone. Tonight, we gather to celebrate the achievements of our teams in driving lean service excellence. Over the past year, we have embarked on a journey of continuous improvement, striving to optimize our service delivery processes and deliver exceptional value to our customers."

James joined her on stage, a broad smile on his face, "Tonight, we honor those individuals and teams who have demonstrated outstanding commitment to lean principles and have made significant contributions to our organization's success. Their dedication, creativity, and passion for excellence have truly set them apart."

Recognizing Lean Service Excellence:

Sarah and James presented awards to individuals and teams who had excelled in various aspects of lean service excellence:

1. **Service Innovation Award:** Presented to the team that implemented the most innovative lean solution to improve service delivery and customer satisfaction.
2. **Continuous Improvement Award:** Recognizing the team that demonstrated the most significant improvements in service quality, efficiency, and customer experi-

ence through continuous improvement initiatives.
3. **Employee Engagement Award:** Given to the team that showed exceptional commitment to engaging employees in the lean process and empowering them to drive improvement in service delivery.
4. **Customer Satisfaction Award:** Awarded to the team that achieved the highest levels of customer satisfaction and loyalty through their dedication to delivering exceptional service.
5. **Leadership Excellence Award:** Presented to the leader who demonstrated outstanding leadership in driving lean initiatives and fostering a culture of continuous improvement within their team or department.
6. **Overall Excellence Award:** The highest honor, given to the individual or team that exemplified excellence in all aspects of lean service delivery, including innovation, continuous improvement, employee engagement, and customer satisfaction.

Celebrating Success:

As each award recipient took the stage to accept their award, the audience erupted into applause, recognizing their dedication and achievements. Sarah and James congratulated each winner, highlighting their contributions to lean service excellence and the positive impact they had made on the organization and its customers.

Inspiring the Future:

In her closing remarks, Sarah inspired the audience to continue their pursuit of lean service excellence, "Tonight, we celebrate the achievements of our teams, but our journey does not end here. Let us be inspired by their example and continue to push the boundaries of what is possible. Together, we can achieve even greater heights of excellence in service delivery."

James echoed her sentiments, "Let us carry the spirit of lean service excellence with us as we embark on the next phase of our journey. With dedication, determination, and a commitment to continuous improvement, there is no limit to what we can achieve."

Conclusion: A Legacy of Excellence

As the event concluded, the audience departed with a renewed sense of purpose and determination to uphold the legacy of lean service excellence. Inspired by the achievements of their peers, they returned to their teams and departments, ready to continue their pursuit of excellence in service delivery and drive continuous improvement in all that they do.

12

Chapter 12: Lean in Healthcare

Lean Principles for Healthcare

In the boardroom at Metropolitan Hospital, Dr. Sofia Garcia and Dr. Michael Chen led a presentation on the application of lean principles in healthcare. Hospital administrators, physicians, and healthcare professionals gathered eagerly, recognizing the potential for lean methodologies to transform healthcare delivery and improve patient outcomes.

Dr. Garcia began, her voice confident and authoritative, "Good morning, everyone. Today, we're going to explore how lean principles can revolutionize healthcare delivery and enhance patient care. While lean methodologies have long been associated with manufacturing and service industries, they offer tremendous opportunities for improvement in healthcare settings as well."

Dr. Chen nodded in agreement, "By applying lean principles such as waste reduction, continuous improvement, and patient-centered care, we can streamline our processes, eliminate inefficiencies, and deliver higher quality care to our patients. Let's delve into the world of lean healthcare together."

Lean Principles for Healthcare:

Dr. Garcia introduced the key lean principles for healthcare and their applications, "Lean principles provide healthcare organizations with a systematic approach to improving patient care and operational efficiency. Some of the key lean principles for healthcare include:

1. **Patient-Centered Care:** Patient-centered care is the cornerstone of lean healthcare. By focusing on the needs and preferences of patients, healthcare organizations can deliver personalized care that is tailored to each individual's unique circumstances and preferences.
2. **Value Stream Mapping:** Value Stream Mapping is a visual tool used to analyze and map the flow of patients, information, and materials through healthcare processes. By identifying value-added and non-value-added activities, healthcare organizations can streamline processes and eliminate waste.
3. **Standardized Work:** Standardized Work involves documenting and following standardized procedures and protocols for delivering healthcare services. By establishing clear guidelines and best practices, healthcare organizations can ensure consistency, quality, and safety in patient care.
4. **Continuous Improvement:** Continuous Improvement is a fundamental principle of lean healthcare. By empowering frontline staff to identify problems, propose

solutions, and implement changes, healthcare organizations can drive continuous improvement in patient care and operational efficiency.
5. **Just-In-Time (JIT) Delivery:** Just-In-Time (JIT) Delivery involves delivering the right care, in the right place, at the right time. By minimizing wait times, reducing delays, and optimizing resource utilization, healthcare organizations can improve patient flow and efficiency.
6. **Respect for People:** Respect for People is a core value of lean healthcare. By fostering a culture of trust, collaboration, and empowerment, healthcare organizations can engage frontline staff in the improvement process and leverage their expertise to drive positive change."

Interactive Discussion:

Dr. Garcia and Dr. Chen facilitated an interactive discussion where hospital administrators, physicians, and healthcare professionals shared their experiences and insights on applying lean principles in healthcare. Participants exchanged ideas, discussed challenges, and brainstormed innovative solutions to improve patient care and operational efficiency.

Conclusion: Transforming Healthcare Delivery

As the presentation concluded, Dr. Garcia and Dr. Chen encouraged the audience to embrace lean principles and apply them in their daily work. "By adopting lean principles and fostering a culture of continuous improvement, we can transform healthcare delivery and improve patient outcomes," Dr. Garcia said.

Dr. Chen nodded in agreement, "Let's commit ourselves to the journey of lean healthcare and work together to deliver the highest quality care to our patients. With dedication, collaboration, and a commitment to excellence, there is no limit to what we can achieve."

The hospital administrators, physicians, and healthcare professionals left the boardroom feeling inspired and motivated, ready to apply lean principles to their practice and drive positive change in healthcare delivery. With a renewed focus on patient-centered care and continuous improvement, Metropolitan Hospital was well-positioned to lead the way in lean healthcare excellence.

Case Studies: Lean Healthcare Success Stories

In the conference room at Metropolitan Hospital, Dr. Sofia Garcia and Dr. Michael Chen presented a series of case studies highlighting successful implementations of lean principles in healthcare. Hospital administrators, physicians, and healthcare professionals gathered eagerly, eager to learn from real-world examples of lean healthcare excellence.

Dr. Garcia began, her voice filled with enthusiasm, "Good afternoon, everyone. Today, we're going to explore some inspiring case studies that demonstrate the transformative power of lean principles in healthcare. From improving patient flow to reducing medication errors, these success stories showcase the tremendous impact that lean methodologies can have on patient care and operational efficiency."

Dr. Chen nodded in agreement, "By studying these case studies, we can gain valuable insights into how lean principles can be applied in healthcare settings to drive positive change and deliver better outcomes for our patients. Let's dive into these success stories together."

Case Study 1: Improving Emergency Department

Efficiency

Dr. Garcia introduced the first case study, "Our first success story takes us to St. Mary's Hospital, where they implemented lean principles to improve efficiency in their emergency department. By streamlining triage processes, optimizing patient flow, and implementing standardized work protocols, they were able to reduce wait times, increase patient satisfaction, and improve staff morale."

Case Study 2: Reducing Medication Errors

Dr. Chen presented the second case study, "Next, we have the story of Mercy Hospital, where they applied lean principles to reduce medication errors and improve patient safety. By implementing visual management tools, standardizing medication administration procedures, and providing staff with training and support, they were able to significantly reduce medication errors and improve patient outcomes."

Case Study 3: Enhancing Operating Room Efficiency

Dr. Garcia continued with the third case study, "Our final success story comes from Johns Hopkins Hospital, where they focused on enhancing efficiency in their operating rooms. By implementing lean principles such as value stream mapping, standardized work, and continuous improvement initiatives, they were able to reduce turnover times, increase surgical throughput, and improve patient flow."

Interactive Discussion: Learning from Success

Dr. Garcia and Dr. Chen facilitated an interactive discussion where hospital administrators, physicians, and healthcare professionals shared their insights and reflections on the case studies presented. Participants discussed the key takeaways, identified opportunities for applying lean principles in their own practice, and brainstormed innovative solutions to improve patient care and operational efficiency.

Conclusion: Inspiring Change

As the discussion concluded, Dr. Garcia and Dr. Chen encouraged the audience to draw inspiration from the case studies presented and apply lean principles in their daily work. "By embracing lean methodologies and fostering a culture of continuous improvement, we can drive positive change and deliver better outcomes for our patients," Dr. Garcia said.

Dr. Chen nodded in agreement, "Let's commit ourselves to the journey of lean healthcare and work together to create a healthcare system that is safer, more efficient, and more patient-centered. With dedication, collaboration, and a commitment to excellence, we can achieve great things."

The hospital administrators, physicians, and healthcare professionals left the conference room feeling inspired and motivated, ready to apply the lessons learned from the case studies to their own practice. With a renewed focus on lean principles and continuous improvement, Metropolitan Hospital was well-positioned to lead the way in lean healthcare excellence.

Lean Tools for Healthcare Improvement

In the training room at Metropolitan Hospital, Dr. Sofia Garcia and Dr. Michael Chen conducted a workshop on the various lean tools available for healthcare improvement. Hospital administrators, physicians, and healthcare professionals gathered eagerly, ready to learn how they could leverage these tools to drive positive change in patient care and operational efficiency.

Dr. Garcia began, her voice resonating with authority,

"Good morning, everyone. Today, we're going to explore a range of lean tools that can be applied in healthcare settings to improve patient care, streamline processes, and enhance operational efficiency. By leveraging these tools effectively, we can drive continuous improvement and deliver better outcomes for our patients."

Dr. Chen nodded in agreement, "From value stream mapping to 5S, these tools offer us valuable frameworks and methodologies for identifying waste, optimizing workflows, and fostering a culture of continuous improvement. Let's delve into the world of lean tools for healthcare improvement together."

Lean Tools for Healthcare Improvement:

Dr. Garcia introduced the key lean tools for healthcare improvement and their applications:

1. **Value Stream Mapping (VSM):** Value Stream Mapping is a visual tool used to analyze and map the flow of patients, information, and materials through healthcare processes. By identifying value-added and non-value-added activities, healthcare organizations can streamline processes, eliminate waste, and improve patient flow.

2. **5S Methodology:** The 5S Methodology (Sort, Set in Order, Shine, Standardize, Sustain) is a systematic approach to workplace organization and cleanliness. By organizing workspaces, standardizing procedures, and fostering a culture of cleanliness and orderliness, healthcare organizations can improve efficiency, reduce errors, and enhance patient safety.

3. **Kaizen Events:** Kaizen Events are focused, short-term improvement projects aimed at solving specific problems

and driving continuous improvement. By bringing together cross-functional teams to identify and implement solutions, healthcare organizations can address issues quickly, improve processes, and engage frontline staff in the improvement process.
4. **Poka-Yoke (Error Proofing):** Poka-Yoke is a technique used to prevent errors and mistakes from occurring in healthcare processes. By designing processes and systems with built-in safeguards and error-proofing mechanisms, healthcare organizations can reduce the risk of errors, improve patient safety, and enhance quality of care.
5. **Standard Work:** Standard Work involves documenting and following standardized procedures and protocols for delivering healthcare services. By establishing clear guidelines and best practices, healthcare organizations can ensure consistency, quality, and safety in patient care.
6. **Root Cause Analysis (RCA):** Root Cause Analysis is a problem-solving technique used to identify the underlying causes of errors, incidents, or issues in healthcare processes. By analyzing root causes and implementing corrective actions, healthcare organizations can prevent recurrence and improve processes.

Interactive Workshop: Hands-On Learning

Dr. Garcia and Dr. Chen facilitated an interactive workshop where hospital administrators, physicians, and healthcare professionals had the opportunity to learn and practice using lean tools in simulated scenarios. Participants worked in teams to apply lean principles and tools to identify waste, streamline processes, and develop solutions to common healthcare challenges.

Conclusion: Empowering Change

As the workshop concluded, Dr. Garcia and Dr. Chen encouraged the audience to apply the lean tools and principles they had learned in their daily work. "By leveraging these tools effectively, we can drive positive change and deliver better outcomes for our patients," Dr. Garcia said.

Dr. Chen nodded in agreement, "Let's commit ourselves to the journey of lean healthcare improvement and work together to create a healthcare system that is safer, more efficient, and more patient-centered. With dedication, collaboration, and a commitment to excellence, we can achieve great things."

The hospital administrators, physicians, and healthcare professionals left the training room feeling empowered and equipped with the knowledge and tools they needed to drive positive change in patient care and operational efficiency. With a renewed focus on lean principles and continuous improvement, Metropolitan Hospital was well-positioned to lead the way in lean healthcare excellence.

Overcoming Resistance in Healthcare

In the auditorium at Metropolitan Hospital, Dr. Sofia Garcia and Dr. Michael Chen led a session focused on addressing resistance to change in healthcare transformation efforts. Hospital administrators, physicians, and healthcare professionals filled the seats, acknowledging the challenges inherent in implementing new methodologies and processes.

Dr. Garcia took the stage, her presence commanding attention, "Good afternoon, everyone. Today, we're going to discuss a topic that is critical to the success of our lean healthcare initiatives: overcoming resistance to change. While the benefits of lean principles are clear, implementing change in a healthcare environment can be met with skepticism and resistance. But with the right strategies and approaches, we can navigate these challenges and drive meaningful transformation."

Dr. Chen nodded in agreement, "By understanding the root causes of resistance and addressing them proactively, we can create a culture that embraces change and fosters continuous improvement. Let's explore how we can overcome resistance in healthcare together."

Overcoming Resistance in Healthcare:

Dr. Garcia introduced strategies for overcoming resistance in healthcare transformation:

1. **Communication and Education:** Effective communication and education are essential for overcoming resistance to change in healthcare. By clearly articulating the rationale for change, addressing concerns, and providing education and training on lean principles, healthcare organizations can build buy-in and support for transformation efforts.
2. **Engagement and Involvement:** Engaging frontline staff and involving them in the change process can help overcome resistance and foster ownership of the transformation. By soliciting input, involving staff in decision-making, and empowering them to drive change, healthcare organizations can harness the collective expertise and knowledge of their workforce.
3. **Leadership Support:** Strong leadership support is

crucial for overcoming resistance to change in healthcare. By demonstrating commitment to lean principles, providing resources and support, and leading by example, healthcare leaders can inspire confidence and create a sense of urgency for change.
4. **Addressing Concerns and Barriers:** Proactively addressing concerns and barriers to change can help mitigate resistance and build momentum for transformation. By identifying potential obstacles, soliciting feedback, and implementing solutions, healthcare organizations can create a supportive environment for change.
5. **Celebrating Successes:** Celebrating successes and recognizing achievements along the way can help maintain momentum and motivation for change. By highlighting the positive impact of lean initiatives, healthcare organizations can inspire confidence and commitment to the transformation process.

Interactive Discussion: Learning from Experience

Dr. Garcia and Dr. Chen facilitated an interactive discussion where hospital administrators, physicians, and healthcare professionals shared their experiences and insights on overcoming resistance to change in healthcare. Participants discussed common challenges, shared best practices, and brainstormed strategies for addressing resistance in their own organizations.

Conclusion: Embracing Change

As the session concluded, Dr. Garcia and Dr. Chen encouraged the audience to embrace change and lean principles in their daily work. "By overcoming resistance and fostering a culture of continuous improvement, we can drive positive change and deliver better outcomes for our patients," Dr. Garcia said.

Dr. Chen nodded in agreement, "Let's commit ourselves to the journey of lean healthcare transformation and work together to create a healthcare system that is safer, more efficient, and more patient-centered. With dedication, collaboration, and a commitment to excellence, we can achieve great things."

The hospital administrators, physicians, and healthcare professionals left the auditorium feeling inspired and empowered, ready to overcome resistance and drive meaningful transformation in healthcare delivery. With a renewed focus on addressing resistance and fostering a culture of continuous improvement, Metropolitan Hospital was well-positioned to lead the way in lean healthcare excellence.

Measuring Lean Success in Healthcare

In the boardroom at Metropolitan Hospital, Dr. Sofia Garcia and Dr. Michael Chen convened a meeting to discuss the measurement of lean success in healthcare. Hospital administrators, physicians, and healthcare professionals gathered around the table, eager to explore how they could quantify the impact of their lean initiatives on patient care and operational efficiency.

Dr. Garcia opened the meeting, her tone focused and determined, "Good morning, everyone. Today, we're going to discuss the critical importance of measuring lean success in healthcare. While our lean initiatives are designed to improve patient care and streamline processes, it's essential that we have metrics in place to evaluate their effectiveness and track our progress over time."

Dr. Chen nodded in agreement, "By establishing clear metrics and performance indicators, we can assess the impact of our lean initiatives, identify areas for improvement, and drive continuous progress. Let's explore how we can measure lean success in healthcare together."

Measuring Lean Success in Healthcare:

Dr. Garcia introduced key metrics and performance indicators for measuring lean success in healthcare:

1. **Operational Efficiency:** Operational efficiency metrics, such as cycle time, lead time, and throughput, can help healthcare organizations assess the efficiency of their processes and identify opportunities for improvement. By reducing wait times, minimizing delays, and optimizing resource utilization, healthcare organizations can improve patient flow and operational performance.
2. **Patient Satisfaction:** Patient satisfaction surveys and feedback mechanisms are essential for measuring the impact of lean initiatives on patient experience and satisfaction. By soliciting feedback from patients and incorporating their input into improvement efforts, healthcare organizations can ensure that their lean initiatives are aligned with patient needs and preferences.
3. **Quality of Care:** Quality of care metrics, such as medication errors, readmission rates, and infection rates, can help healthcare organizations assess the impact of lean initiatives on patient safety and clinical outcomes. By reducing errors, preventing adverse events, and improving clinical outcomes, healthcare organizations can enhance the quality of care they deliver to patients.

4. **Employee Engagement:** Employee engagement surveys and assessments can help healthcare organizations measure the impact of lean initiatives on staff morale, satisfaction, and engagement. By empowering frontline staff, recognizing their contributions, and providing opportunities for professional development, healthcare organizations can foster a culture of engagement and commitment to continuous improvement.
5. **Financial Performance:** Financial performance metrics, such as cost savings, revenue growth, and return on investment (ROI), can help healthcare organizations quantify the financial impact of their lean initiatives. By reducing waste, improving efficiency, and enhancing productivity, healthcare organizations can achieve cost savings and financial sustainability.

Interactive Discussion: Defining Success

Dr. Garcia and Dr. Chen facilitated an interactive discussion where hospital administrators, physicians, and healthcare professionals shared their perspectives on measuring lean success in healthcare. Participants discussed the importance of aligning metrics with organizational goals, establishing benchmarks for success, and continuously monitoring performance to drive improvement.

Conclusion: Driving Continuous Improvement

As the meeting concluded, Dr. Garcia and Dr. Chen emphasized the importance of measuring lean success in healthcare and using data-driven insights to drive continuous improvement. "By establishing clear metrics and performance indicators, we can assess the impact of our lean initiatives and drive meaningful change in patient care and operational efficiency," Dr. Garcia said.

Dr. Chen nodded in agreement, "Let's commit ourselves to the journey of lean healthcare excellence and work together to achieve our goals. With dedication, collaboration, and a commitment to excellence, there is no limit to what we can achieve."

The hospital administrators, physicians, and healthcare professionals left the boardroom feeling motivated and empowered, ready to implement robust measurement systems and drive continuous improvement in patient care and operational efficiency. With a renewed focus on measuring lean success in healthcare, Metropolitan Hospital was well-positioned to lead the way in lean healthcare excellence.

The Future of Lean in Healthcare

In the conference room at Metropolitan Hospital, Dr. Sofia Garcia and Dr. Michael Chen led a discussion on the future of lean in healthcare. Hospital administrators, physicians, and healthcare professionals gathered eagerly, ready to explore the evolving landscape of lean principles and methodologies in healthcare delivery.

Dr. Garcia opened the discussion, her voice filled with anticipation, "Good afternoon, everyone. Today, we're going to explore the exciting possibilities and challenges that lie ahead in the future of lean healthcare. As we continue to navigate a rapidly changing healthcare landscape, it's essential that we stay ahead of the curve and embrace innovations that will drive continuous improvement and deliver better outcomes for our patients."

Dr. Chen nodded in agreement, "By anticipating emerging

trends, leveraging new technologies, and fostering a culture of innovation, we can position ourselves as leaders in lean healthcare excellence. Let's envision the future of lean in healthcare together."

The Future of Lean in Healthcare:

Dr. Garcia introduced key trends and developments shaping the future of lean in healthcare:

1. **Digital Transformation:** Digital transformation is revolutionizing healthcare delivery, offering new opportunities to streamline processes, improve efficiency, and enhance patient care. By leveraging electronic health records, telemedicine, and data analytics, healthcare organizations can optimize workflows, personalize care, and drive better outcomes for patients.
2. **Population Health Management:** Population health management is gaining prominence as healthcare organizations shift their focus from treating individual patients to managing the health of entire populations. By adopting proactive, preventive approaches to healthcare delivery, healthcare organizations can improve population health outcomes, reduce healthcare costs, and enhance the patient experience.
3. **Value-Based Care:** Value-based care models are transforming reimbursement structures and incentivizing healthcare organizations to deliver high-quality, cost-effective care. By aligning financial incentives with patient outcomes and quality metrics, value-based care models encourage healthcare organizations to prioritize value over volume and drive continuous improvement in patient care.

4. **Patient-Centered Care:** Patient-centered care continues to be a guiding principle in lean healthcare, emphasizing the importance of tailoring care to meet the individual needs and preferences of patients. By engaging patients as partners in their care, fostering open communication, and providing compassionate, personalized care, healthcare organizations can improve patient satisfaction, loyalty, and outcomes.
5. **Global Collaboration:** Global collaboration and knowledge sharing are essential for advancing lean principles and methodologies in healthcare. By collaborating with healthcare organizations, research institutions, and industry partners around the world, healthcare organizations can learn from best practices, exchange ideas, and drive innovation in lean healthcare delivery.

Interactive Discussion: Shaping the Future

Dr. Garcia and Dr. Chen facilitated an interactive discussion where hospital administrators, physicians, and healthcare professionals shared their insights and visions for the future of lean in healthcare. Participants discussed the challenges and opportunities presented by emerging trends, identified areas for innovation, and brainstormed strategies for driving continuous improvement in patient care and operational efficiency.

Conclusion: Leading the Way

As the discussion concluded, Dr. Garcia and Dr. Chen emphasized the importance of embracing innovation and staying ahead of the curve in the future of lean healthcare. "By envisioning the future of lean in healthcare and embracing emerging trends and technologies, we can position ourselves as leaders in lean healthcare excellence," Dr. Garcia said.

Dr. Chen nodded in agreement, "Let's commit ourselves to the journey of continuous improvement and innovation in healthcare delivery. With dedication, collaboration, and a commitment to excellence, we can shape the future of lean in healthcare and deliver better outcomes for our patients."

The hospital administrators, physicians, and healthcare professionals left the conference room feeling inspired and energized, ready to embrace the future of lean in healthcare and drive meaningful change in patient care and operational efficiency. With a renewed focus on innovation and continuous improvement, Metropolitan Hospital was well-positioned to lead the way in lean healthcare excellence in the years to come.

13

Chapter 13: Lean in Supply Chain Management

Lean Supply Chain Principles

In the supply chain department at Metropolitan Hospital, a group of supply chain managers and logistics professionals gathered for a workshop on lean supply chain principles. Led by Dr. Sofia Garcia and Dr. Michael Chen, the participants were eager to learn how they could apply lean principles to optimize their supply chain operations.

Dr. Garcia addressed the group, her voice commanding attention, "Good morning, everyone. Today, we're going to explore the foundational principles of lean supply chain management. As the backbone of our organization's operations, the supply chain plays a critical role in delivering high-quality care to our patients. By embracing lean principles, we can streamline our supply chain processes, reduce waste, and enhance efficiency."

Dr. Chen nodded in agreement, "By focusing on value creation, eliminating waste, and fostering collaboration with our suppliers and partners, we can create a lean and agile supply chain that is responsive to the needs of our organization and our patients. Let's delve into the world of lean supply chain principles together."

Lean Supply Chain Principles:

Dr. Garcia introduced key lean supply chain principles and their applications:

1. **Value Stream Mapping:** Value stream mapping is a visual tool used to analyze and map the flow of materials, information, and processes across the supply chain. By identifying value-added and non-value-added activities, supply chain organizations can streamline processes, reduce lead times, and improve efficiency.
2. **Just-in-Time (JIT) Inventory Management:** Just-in-time inventory management aims to minimize inventory levels and reduce waste by delivering materials and products to the right place at the right time. By synchronizing production and delivery schedules with customer demand, supply chain organizations can improve responsiveness, reduce storage costs, and enhance efficiency.
3. **Continuous Improvement:** Continuous improvement is a fundamental principle of lean supply chain management, emphasizing the importance of ongoing refinement and optimization of processes. By empowering employees to identify and implement improvements, supply chain organizations can drive incremental gains in efficiency, quality, and cost-effectiveness.

4. **Supplier Collaboration:** Supplier collaboration involves building strong partnerships and relationships with suppliers to drive mutual success. By sharing information, aligning goals, and collaborating on process improvements, supply chain organizations can reduce lead times, improve product quality, and enhance overall supply chain performance.
5. **Standardized Work:** Standardized work involves documenting and following standardized procedures and protocols for supply chain operations. By establishing clear guidelines and best practices, supply chain organizations can ensure consistency, quality, and efficiency in their processes.

Interactive Workshop: Hands-On Learning

Dr. Garcia and Dr. Chen facilitated an interactive workshop where supply chain managers and logistics professionals had the opportunity to learn and practice applying lean principles in simulated scenarios. Participants worked in teams to analyze supply chain processes, identify opportunities for improvement, and develop solutions to common supply chain challenges.

Conclusion: Driving Supply Chain Excellence

As the workshop concluded, Dr. Garcia and Dr. Chen encouraged the participants to apply the lean supply chain principles they had learned in their daily work. "By embracing lean principles and fostering a culture of continuous improvement, we can create a lean and agile supply chain that delivers value to our organization and our patients," Dr. Garcia said.

Dr. Chen nodded in agreement, "Let's commit ourselves to the journey of lean supply chain excellence and work together to optimize our supply chain operations. With dedication, collaboration, and a commitment to excellence, there is no limit to what we can achieve."

The supply chain managers and logistics professionals left the workshop feeling inspired and empowered, ready to apply lean principles to optimize their supply chain operations and drive value for Metropolitan Hospital. With a renewed focus on lean supply chain principles, Metropolitan Hospital was well-positioned to lead the way in supply chain excellence in healthcare delivery.

Streamlining Supply Chain Processes

In the bustling operations center of Metropolitan Hospital's supply chain department, a team of supply chain managers and logistics professionals gathered to discuss how they could streamline their processes using lean principles. Led by Dr. Sofia Garcia and Dr. Michael Chen, the team was eager to identify opportunities for improvement and enhance the efficiency of their supply chain operations.

Dr. Garcia addressed the team, her voice filled with determination, "Good afternoon, everyone. Today, we're going to focus on streamlining our supply chain processes to reduce waste, improve efficiency, and enhance our overall performance. By embracing lean principles and fostering a culture of continuous improvement, we can optimize our processes and deliver value to our organization and our patients."

Dr. Chen nodded in agreement, "By analyzing our current processes, identifying bottlenecks, and implementing solutions to streamline workflows, we can create a lean and agile supply chain that is responsive to the needs of our organization. Let's roll up our sleeves and get to work."

Streamlining Supply Chain Processes:

Dr. Garcia introduced key strategies for streamlining supply chain processes and their applications:

1. **Value Stream Analysis:** Value stream analysis involves mapping the flow of materials, information, and processes across the supply chain to identify inefficiencies and opportunities for improvement. By analyzing value streams, supply chain organizations can eliminate waste, reduce lead times, and optimize workflows.
2. **Standard Work:** Standard work involves documenting and following standardized procedures and protocols for supply chain operations. By establishing clear guidelines and best practices, supply chain organizations can ensure consistency, quality, and efficiency in their processes.
3. **Automation and Technology:** Automation and technology solutions, such as robotic process automation (RPA), warehouse management systems (WMS), and inventory management software, can help streamline supply chain processes and reduce manual intervention. By automating routine tasks and leveraging data analytics, supply chain organizations can improve accuracy, reduce errors, and enhance efficiency.
4. **Cross-Functional Collaboration:** Cross-functional collaboration involves breaking down silos and fostering collaboration between different departments and teams within the organization. By involving stakeholders from across the organization in supply chain planning

and decision-making, supply chain organizations can improve communication, coordination, and alignment of goals.

5. **Continuous Improvement:** Continuous improvement is a fundamental principle of lean supply chain management, emphasizing the importance of ongoing refinement and optimization of processes. By empowering employees to identify and implement improvements, supply chain organizations can drive incremental gains in efficiency, quality, and cost-effectiveness.

Interactive Workshop: Process Improvement

Dr. Garcia and Dr. Chen facilitated an interactive workshop where supply chain managers and logistics professionals had the opportunity to analyze their current processes, identify opportunities for improvement, and develop solutions to streamline workflows. Participants worked collaboratively to brainstorm ideas, prioritize initiatives, and create action plans for process improvement.

Conclusion: Driving Efficiency

As the workshop concluded, Dr. Garcia and Dr. Chen commended the team for their efforts and commitment to driving efficiency in supply chain operations. "By embracing lean principles and implementing solutions to streamline our processes, we can create a lean and agile supply chain that delivers value to our organization and our patients," Dr. Garcia said.

Dr. Chen nodded in agreement, "Let's continue to work together to identify opportunities for improvement and drive efficiency in our supply chain operations. With dedication, collaboration, and a commitment to excellence, there is no limit to what we can achieve."

The supply chain managers and logistics professionals left the operations center feeling energized and motivated, ready to implement their action plans and drive efficiency in Metropolitan Hospital's supply chain operations. With a renewed focus on streamlining processes, Metropolitan Hospital was well-positioned to optimize its supply chain and deliver value for the organization and its patients.

Case Studies: Lean Supply Chain Success

In the conference room at Metropolitan Hospital, a group of supply chain managers and logistics professionals gathered to learn from real-world examples of lean supply chain success. Led by Dr. Sofia Garcia and Dr. Michael Chen, the participants were eager to gain insights and inspiration from organizations that had successfully implemented lean principles in their supply chain operations.

Dr. Garcia addressed the group, her voice filled with enthusiasm, "Good morning, everyone. Today, we're going to explore case studies of organizations that have achieved remarkable success through the implementation of lean principles in their supply chain operations. By learning from their experiences and best practices, we can gain valuable insights to apply to our own supply chain efforts."

Dr. Chen nodded in agreement, "By studying these success stories, we can identify common strategies, challenges, and lessons learned that can inform our approach to lean supply chain management. Let's dive into the case studies and uncover the secrets of their success."

Case Studies: Lean Supply Chain Success

Dr. Garcia presented several case studies of organizations that had achieved success through the implementation of lean principles in their supply chain operations:

1. **Toyota:** Toyota is renowned for its pioneering approach to lean manufacturing and supply chain management, exemplified by its Toyota Production System (TPS). By implementing principles such as just-in-time inventory management, continuous improvement, and respect for people, Toyota has achieved exceptional levels of efficiency, quality, and responsiveness in its supply chain operations.
2. **Amazon:** Amazon has revolutionized the retail industry with its innovative approach to supply chain management, driven by data analytics, automation, and customer-centricity. By leveraging advanced technology and logistics capabilities, Amazon has built a highly efficient and flexible supply chain that enables rapid order fulfillment and delivery, meeting the ever-changing needs of its customers.
3. **Procter & Gamble:** Procter & Gamble (P&G) has embraced lean principles to optimize its supply chain operations and drive efficiency and agility. By collaborating closely with suppliers, implementing demand-driven production processes, and leveraging advanced analytics and forecasting techniques, P&G has reduced lead times, inventory levels, and costs while improving service levels and customer satisfaction.
4. **Zara:** Zara, the Spanish fast-fashion retailer, has disrupted the fashion industry with its agile and responsive supply chain model. By vertically integrating design,

production, and distribution processes, and leveraging real-time data and feedback from stores and customers, Zara has shortened lead times, reduced inventory risk, and increased sales and profitability.
5. **Walmart:** Walmart has leveraged its scale and supply chain expertise to drive efficiency and cost savings throughout its global supply chain network. By implementing strategies such as cross-docking, vendor-managed inventory, and advanced logistics technologies, Walmart has optimized its supply chain operations, reduced costs, and improved product availability and customer satisfaction.

Interactive Discussion: Key Takeaways

Dr. Garcia and Dr. Chen facilitated an interactive discussion where supply chain managers and logistics professionals shared their insights and key takeaways from the case studies. Participants discussed the strategies and practices that had contributed to the success of each organization and brainstormed ideas for applying similar approaches in their own supply chain operations.

Conclusion: Learning and Application

As the discussion concluded, Dr. Garcia and Dr. Chen encouraged the participants to reflect on the lessons learned from the case studies and apply them to their own supply chain efforts. "By learning from the successes of others and adapting their strategies to our own context, we can drive meaningful improvement in our supply chain operations," Dr. Garcia said.

Dr. Chen nodded in agreement, "Let's continue to learn, innovate, and collaborate as we work towards creating a lean and agile supply chain that delivers value to our organization and our patients."

The supply chain managers and logistics professionals left the conference room feeling inspired and motivated, armed with new insights and strategies to enhance their supply chain operations. With a renewed focus on lean principles and best practices, Metropolitan Hospital was well-positioned to optimize its supply chain and drive value for the organization and its patients.

Tools for Lean Supply Chain Management

In the training room of Metropolitan Hospital's supply chain department, a group of supply chain managers and logistics professionals gathered to explore the tools and techniques used in lean supply chain management. Led by Dr. Sofia Garcia and Dr. Michael Chen, the participants were eager to learn how they could leverage these tools to optimize their supply chain operations.

Dr. Garcia addressed the group, her voice echoing with excitement, "Good afternoon, everyone. Today, we're going to explore the various tools and techniques used in lean supply chain management. By understanding these tools and how they can be applied in our own operations, we can drive efficiency, reduce waste, and enhance the performance of our supply chain."

Dr. Chen nodded in agreement, "By leveraging these tools effectively, we can identify opportunities for improvement, streamline processes, and create a lean and agile supply chain that delivers value to our organization and our patients. Let's dive into the world of lean supply chain tools together."

Tools for Lean Supply Chain Management:

Dr. Garcia introduced several key tools and techniques used in lean supply chain management:

1. **Kaizen:** Kaizen, or continuous improvement, is a fundamental principle of lean management. By empowering employees to identify and implement small, incremental improvements in their work processes, supply chain organizations can drive continuous improvement and optimize their operations over time.
2. **Kanban:** Kanban is a visual scheduling system used to manage inventory levels and production processes. By using visual cues, such as cards or boards, to signal when materials or tasks should be replenished or completed, supply chain organizations can reduce lead times, minimize waste, and improve workflow efficiency.
3. **5S:** 5S is a methodology for organizing and standardizing workspaces to improve efficiency, safety, and quality. By implementing the principles of Sort, Set in Order, Shine, Standardize, and Sustain, supply chain organizations can create a clean, organized, and efficient work environment that supports lean operations.
4. **Poka-Yoke:** Poka-Yoke, or mistake-proofing, involves designing processes and systems to prevent errors and defects from occurring. By implementing poka-yoke techniques, such as checklists, visual cues, and error-proofing devices, supply chain organizations can reduce errors, improve quality, and enhance productivity.
5. **Value Stream Mapping:** Value stream mapping is a visual tool used to analyze and map the flow of materials, information, and processes across the supply chain. By

identifying value-added and non-value-added activities, supply chain organizations can eliminate waste, reduce lead times, and optimize workflows.

Interactive Workshop: Hands-On Learning

Dr. Garcia and Dr. Chen facilitated an interactive workshop where supply chain managers and logistics professionals had the opportunity to learn and practice using lean tools in simulated scenarios. Participants worked in teams to analyze supply chain processes, identify opportunities for improvement, and develop solutions using lean tools and techniques.

Conclusion: Driving Efficiency

As the workshop concluded, Dr. Garcia and Dr. Chen commended the participants for their engagement and enthusiasm in exploring lean tools for supply chain management. "By leveraging these tools effectively, we can drive efficiency, reduce waste, and create a lean and agile supply chain that delivers value to our organization and our patients," Dr. Garcia said.

Dr. Chen nodded in agreement, "Let's continue to apply these tools and techniques in our daily work and drive continuous improvement in our supply chain operations. With dedication, collaboration, and a commitment to excellence, there is no limit to what we can achieve."

The supply chain managers and logistics professionals left the training room feeling empowered and equipped with new tools and techniques to enhance their supply chain operations. With a renewed focus on lean principles and best practices, Metropolitan Hospital was well-positioned to optimize its supply chain and drive value for the organization and its patients.

Overcoming Challenges in Lean Supply Chains

In the strategy meeting of Metropolitan Hospital's supply chain department, a sense of determination filled the air as supply chain managers and logistics professionals gathered to address the challenges they faced in implementing lean principles. Led by Dr. Sofia Garcia and Dr. Michael Chen, the team was ready to confront obstacles head-on and find solutions to overcome them.

Dr. Garcia addressed the group, her voice steady and reassuring, "Good morning, everyone. Today, we're going to discuss the challenges we face in implementing lean principles in our supply chain operations and explore strategies to overcome them. By identifying these challenges and working together to find solutions, we can ensure the success of our lean supply chain initiatives."

Dr. Chen nodded in agreement, "By acknowledging and addressing these challenges proactively, we can navigate the path to lean supply chain excellence and drive meaningful improvement in our operations. Let's face these challenges with determination and perseverance."

Overcoming Challenges in Lean Supply Chains:

Dr. Garcia highlighted several common challenges faced by supply chain organizations in implementing lean principles:

1. **Resistance to Change:** Resistance to change is a common challenge encountered when implementing lean principles in supply chain operations. Employees may be reluctant to adopt new processes or technologies,

fearing disruption or loss of control. By fostering open communication, providing training and support, and emphasizing the benefits of lean principles, supply chain organizations can overcome resistance and gain buy-in from employees.

2. **Lack of Leadership Support:** Lack of leadership support can hinder the successful implementation of lean principles in supply chain operations. Without strong leadership commitment and sponsorship, initiatives may lack direction, resources, and accountability. By engaging senior leadership, aligning lean initiatives with organizational goals, and demonstrating the value of lean principles through tangible results, supply chain organizations can secure the support and commitment needed for success.

3. **Complexity and Variability:** Supply chain operations are often complex and subject to variability, making it challenging to implement lean principles effectively. Factors such as fluctuating demand, diverse product portfolios, and global supply chains can introduce uncertainty and disrupt lean processes. By leveraging tools such as demand forecasting, inventory optimization, and risk management strategies, supply chain organizations can mitigate complexity and variability and improve the stability and predictability of their operations.

4. **Supply Chain Disruptions:** Supply chain disruptions, such as natural disasters, geopolitical events, and supplier failures, can disrupt lean operations and undermine supply chain performance. By implementing strategies such as supply chain risk management, business continuity planning, and agile supply chain practices, supply chain

organizations can build resilience and respond effectively to disruptions, minimizing their impact on operations and customers.

Interactive Discussion: Collaborative Solutions

Dr. Garcia and Dr. Chen facilitated an interactive discussion where supply chain managers and logistics professionals shared their experiences and insights on overcoming challenges in lean supply chain management. Participants brainstormed collaborative solutions and strategies to address the challenges they faced, drawing on their collective expertise and creativity.

Conclusion: Moving Forward with Resilience

As the discussion concluded, Dr. Garcia and Dr. Chen commended the team for their thoughtful contributions and commitment to overcoming challenges in lean supply chain management. "By facing these challenges with resilience and determination, we can navigate the path to lean supply chain excellence and drive meaningful improvement in our operations," Dr. Garcia said.

Dr. Chen nodded in agreement, "Let's continue to work together, support each other, and learn from our experiences as we journey towards lean supply chain excellence. With perseverance and collaboration, there is no challenge we cannot overcome."

The supply chain managers and logistics professionals left the strategy meeting feeling inspired and empowered, ready to tackle challenges head-on and drive improvement in Metropolitan Hospital's supply chain operations. With a renewed sense of resilience and determination, Metropolitan Hospital was well-equipped to overcome obstacles and achieve success in its lean supply chain initiatives.

Future Trends in Lean Supply Chain Management

In the innovation lab of Metropolitan Hospital's supply chain department, a group of supply chain managers and logistics professionals gathered to explore the future trends shaping the landscape of lean supply chain management. Led by Dr. Sofia Garcia and Dr. Michael Chen, the team was eager to stay ahead of the curve and anticipate the challenges and opportunities that lay ahead.

Dr. Garcia addressed the group, her voice tinged with excitement, "Good morning, everyone. Today, we're going to explore the future trends in lean supply chain management and envision the possibilities for innovation and improvement in our operations. By staying informed and proactive, we can position ourselves for success in the rapidly evolving world of supply chain management."

Dr. Chen nodded in agreement, "By embracing emerging technologies, evolving customer expectations, and shifting market dynamics, we can adapt and thrive in the future of lean supply chain management. Let's explore these trends together and unlock new opportunities for innovation and growth."

Future Trends in Lean Supply Chain Management:
Dr. Garcia outlined several key future trends shaping the landscape of lean supply chain management:

1. **Digital Transformation:** Digital transformation is revolutionizing supply chain management, enabling real-time visibility, predictive analytics, and automation. Technologies such as Internet of Things (IoT), artificial

intelligence (AI), and blockchain are transforming how supply chain organizations manage inventory, track shipments, and optimize operations, driving efficiency and agility.

2. **Sustainability and Environmental Responsibility:** Sustainability and environmental responsibility are becoming increasingly important considerations in supply chain management. Organizations are adopting lean principles to minimize waste, reduce carbon footprint, and optimize resource utilization throughout the supply chain, aligning with consumer preferences and regulatory requirements.

3. **Resilience and Risk Management:** Resilience and risk management are critical considerations in supply chain management, particularly in the face of global disruptions and uncertainties. Supply chain organizations are implementing strategies such as supply chain mapping, scenario planning, and supplier diversification to build resilience and mitigate risks, ensuring continuity of operations and customer satisfaction.

4. **Customer-Centricity and Personalization:** Customer-centricity and personalization are driving new expectations and demands in supply chain management. Organizations are leveraging lean principles to enable greater customization, flexibility, and responsiveness in their supply chain operations, meeting the unique needs and preferences of individual customers and market segments.

Interactive Discussion: Envisioning the Future

Dr. Garcia and Dr. Chen facilitated an interactive discussion where supply chain managers and logistics professionals shared their insights and visions for the future of lean supply chain management. Participants brainstormed ideas for leveraging emerging technologies, addressing sustainability challenges, and enhancing customer-centricity in their supply chain operations.

Conclusion: Embracing Innovation

As the discussion concluded, Dr. Garcia and Dr. Chen commended the team for their forward-thinking approach and enthusiasm for innovation in lean supply chain management. "By embracing these future trends and harnessing the power of innovation, we can drive meaningful improvement and create a lean and agile supply chain that delivers value to our organization and our patients," Dr. Garcia said.

Dr. Chen nodded in agreement, "Let's continue to stay informed, proactive, and collaborative as we navigate the evolving landscape of lean supply chain management. With innovation and agility, there is no limit to what we can achieve."

The supply chain managers and logistics professionals left the innovation lab feeling inspired and energized, ready to embrace the future of lean supply chain management and unlock new opportunities for innovation and growth. With a shared vision for the future, Metropolitan Hospital was well-positioned to lead the way in lean supply chain excellence in healthcare delivery.

14

Chapter 14: Digital Transformation and Lean

The Role of Technology in Lean

In the Digital Innovation Center of Metropolitan Hospital, a team of healthcare professionals and technology experts gathered to explore the intersection of digital transformation and lean principles. Led by Dr. Sofia Garcia and Dr. Michael Chen, the team was eager to uncover how technology could enhance lean practices and drive efficiency in healthcare delivery.

Dr. Garcia addressed the group, her voice filled with anticipation, "Good morning, everyone. Today, we're going to explore the role of technology in lean principles and how digital transformation can revolutionize healthcare delivery. By leveraging technology effectively, we can enhance our lean practices and improve patient outcomes."

Dr. Chen nodded in agreement, "Technology has the power to streamline processes, enhance visibility, and enable data-driven decision-making in healthcare. Let's explore how we can harness the potential of technology to drive lean transformation and deliver value to our patients."

The Role of Technology in Lean:

Dr. Garcia outlined the pivotal role of technology in enabling lean practices and driving continuous improvement:

1. **Data Analytics:** Data analytics plays a crucial role in lean practices by providing insights into operational performance, identifying areas for improvement, and supporting data-driven decision-making. By leveraging advanced analytics tools and techniques, healthcare organizations can analyze large volumes of data, detect patterns, and optimize processes to enhance efficiency and quality of care.
2. **Automation:** Automation enables the automation of routine tasks, reduces manual intervention, and streamlines workflows in healthcare operations. Technologies such as robotic process automation (RPA), artificial intelligence (AI), and machine learning (ML) can automate repetitive tasks, improve accuracy, and free up healthcare professionals to focus on higher-value activities, driving efficiency and productivity.
3. **Telemedicine:** Telemedicine enables remote diagnosis, monitoring, and treatment of patients, eliminating the need for in-person visits and reducing healthcare costs and waiting times. By leveraging telemedicine technologies, healthcare organizations can expand access to care, improve patient engagement, and enhance the efficiency of healthcare delivery, particularly in remote or underserved areas.

4. **Electronic Health Records (EHR):** Electronic health records (EHR) digitize patient health information, streamline documentation, and facilitate information sharing across healthcare settings. By implementing EHR systems, healthcare organizations can improve care coordination, reduce medical errors, and enhance patient safety, leading to better outcomes and experiences for patients.

Interactive Discussion: Exploring Possibilities

Dr. Garcia and Dr. Chen facilitated an interactive discussion where healthcare professionals and technology experts shared their insights and ideas for leveraging technology in lean practices. Participants brainstormed innovative solutions, discussed best practices, and explored opportunities for collaboration to drive digital transformation and lean excellence in healthcare delivery.

Conclusion: Embracing Innovation

As the discussion concluded, Dr. Garcia and Dr. Chen commended the team for their enthusiasm and creativity in exploring the role of technology in lean practices. "By embracing technology and leveraging digital transformation, we can enhance our lean practices, improve patient outcomes, and drive continuous improvement in healthcare delivery," Dr. Garcia said.

Dr. Chen nodded in agreement, "Let's continue to innovate, collaborate, and embrace digital transformation as we work towards delivering high-quality, patient-centered care. With technology as our ally, there is no limit to what we can achieve."

The healthcare professionals and technology experts left

the Digital Innovation Center feeling inspired and motivated, ready to harness the power of technology to drive lean transformation and deliver value to patients. With a shared vision for the future, Metropolitan Hospital was well-positioned to lead the way in digital innovation and lean excellence in healthcare delivery.

Integrating Digital Tools with Lean Practices

In the Lean Implementation Office of Metropolitan Hospital, a team of lean practitioners and digital experts gathered to explore the integration of digital tools with lean practices. Led by Dr. Sofia Garcia and Dr. Michael Chen, the team was eager to uncover synergies between technology and lean principles to drive efficiency and innovation in healthcare delivery.

Dr. Garcia addressed the group, her voice filled with determination, "Good morning, everyone. Today, we're going to explore how we can integrate digital tools with lean practices to enhance our operations and improve patient care. By leveraging technology effectively, we can optimize processes, empower our teams, and deliver value to our patients."

Dr. Chen nodded in agreement, "Integrating digital tools with lean practices has the potential to revolutionize healthcare delivery, enabling real-time insights, automation, and continuous improvement. Let's explore how we can bridge technology and lean principles to drive transformation in our organization."

Integrating Digital Tools with Lean Practices:

Dr. Garcia outlined several strategies for integrating digital tools with lean practices to drive efficiency and innovation:

CHAPTER 14: DIGITAL TRANSFORMATION AND LEAN

1. **Process Automation:** Process automation involves leveraging digital tools such as robotic process automation (RPA) and workflow management systems to automate routine tasks and streamline processes. By automating repetitive and manual tasks, healthcare organizations can improve efficiency, reduce errors, and free up staff time for higher-value activities, enabling lean practices to thrive.
2. **Real-Time Data Analytics:** Real-time data analytics enables healthcare organizations to analyze and act on data in real-time, providing insights into operational performance, patient outcomes, and resource utilization. By leveraging advanced analytics tools and techniques, healthcare organizations can identify trends, detect anomalies, and make data-driven decisions to drive continuous improvement and enhance lean practices.
3. **Collaborative Platforms:** Collaborative platforms such as digital dashboards, communication tools, and project management software facilitate collaboration and communication among teams, enabling cross-functional collaboration and knowledge sharing. By providing a centralized platform for sharing information, tracking progress, and coordinating activities, collaborative platforms support lean practices such as teamwork, transparency, and continuous improvement.
4. **Digital Work Instructions:** Digital work instructions digitize standard work processes and procedures, providing step-by-step guidance and visual aids to frontline staff. By digitizing work instructions, healthcare organizations can standardize processes, reduce variability, and improve consistency and quality of care, aligning

with lean principles such as standardization and visual management.

Interactive Workshop: Exploring Possibilities

Dr. Garcia and Dr. Chen facilitated an interactive workshop where lean practitioners and digital experts collaborated to explore opportunities for integrating digital tools with lean practices. Participants brainstormed ideas, shared best practices, and identified potential use cases for digital tools to enhance lean practices and drive transformation in healthcare delivery.

Conclusion: Driving Innovation

As the workshop concluded, Dr. Garcia and Dr. Chen commended the team for their creativity and collaboration in exploring the integration of digital tools with lean practices. "By embracing digital transformation and leveraging technology to support lean practices, we can drive innovation, improve efficiency, and deliver value to our patients," Dr. Garcia said.

Dr. Chen nodded in agreement, "Let's continue to explore, experiment, and innovate as we bridge technology and lean principles to drive transformation in healthcare delivery. With dedication and collaboration, there is no limit to what we can achieve."

The lean practitioners and digital experts left the Lean Implementation Office feeling inspired and energized, ready to harness the power of digital tools to enhance lean practices and drive innovation in healthcare delivery. With a shared vision for the future, Metropolitan Hospital was well-equipped to lead the way in integrating technology and lean principles to deliver high-quality, patient-centered care.

Case Studies: Digital Lean Success Stories

In the bustling conference room of Metropolitan Hospital, a diverse group of healthcare professionals, IT experts, and lean practitioners gathered for a special session. The atmosphere was charged with excitement as Dr. Sofia Garcia and Dr. Michael Chen prepared to present case studies showcasing successful integrations of digital tools with lean practices.

Dr. Garcia began, her voice resonating with enthusiasm, "Good afternoon, everyone. Today, we are thrilled to share inspiring case studies that highlight the successful integration of digital tools with lean practices. These stories demonstrate the transformative power of technology in enhancing lean principles and driving remarkable improvements in healthcare delivery."

Dr. Chen added, "By learning from these success stories, we can gain valuable insights and apply best practices to our own efforts here at Metropolitan Hospital. Let's dive into these real-world examples and explore the innovative solutions that have led to outstanding results."

Case Study 1: Automating Patient Scheduling at Riverside Medical Center

Dr. Garcia introduced the first case study, focusing on Riverside Medical Center's efforts to automate patient scheduling. The center had faced challenges with manual scheduling processes, leading to inefficiencies and patient dissatisfaction.

"Riverside Medical Center implemented a digital scheduling platform integrated with their electronic health record (EHR) system," Dr. Garcia explained. "This automation streamlined the scheduling process, reduced errors, and improved patient satisfaction. By leveraging real-time data analytics, they could also optimize appointment slots and reduce wait times."

A video clip played, showing the bustling corridors of Riverside Medical Center and testimonials from staff and patients who praised the new system. The room buzzed with appreciation for the practical application of digital lean principles.

Case Study 2: Real-Time Inventory Management at Greenfield Pharmacy

Dr. Chen took the stage to present the next case study, highlighting Greenfield Pharmacy's innovative approach to inventory management. The pharmacy had struggled with stockouts and overstock issues, impacting patient care and operational efficiency.

"Greenfield Pharmacy implemented a real-time inventory management system using IoT sensors and data analytics," Dr. Chen explained. "This system provided real-time visibility into inventory levels, enabling them to track usage patterns and optimize stock levels. As a result, they significantly reduced stockouts and minimized waste."

A detailed infographic displayed the dramatic improvements in inventory metrics, and a testimonial video from Greenfield Pharmacy's staff underscored the positive impact on their workflow and patient service.

Case Study 3: Enhancing Patient Care Coordination at Horizon Health

Dr. Garcia continued with a case study from Horizon Health, which focused on enhancing patient care coordination through digital collaboration tools.

"Horizon Health adopted a collaborative platform that integrated communication tools, digital work instructions, and project management software," Dr. Garcia said. "This platform facilitated seamless communication among care teams, standardized procedures, and improved care coordination. The result was enhanced patient outcomes and increased staff satisfaction."

A series of before-and-after charts illustrated the improvements in patient care metrics, and a video clip showcased the platform in action, with staff members highlighting its impact on their daily routines.

Case Study 4: Remote Monitoring and Telehealth at Lakeside Clinic

Dr. Chen introduced the final case study, showcasing Lakeside Clinic's success with remote monitoring and telehealth services.

"Lakeside Clinic implemented telehealth platforms and remote monitoring devices to extend care beyond the clinic walls," Dr. Chen explained. "Patients could consult with their healthcare providers remotely, and clinicians could monitor chronic conditions in real-time. This approach improved access to care, reduced hospital readmissions, and enhanced patient engagement."

A series of patient testimonials played, sharing heartfelt stories of how telehealth had positively impacted their lives. The audience was visibly moved, appreciating the human side of digital transformation.

Interactive Discussion: Learning and Applying Best Practices

Dr. Garcia and Dr. Chen facilitated an interactive discussion, encouraging attendees to share their thoughts and ideas on applying these success stories at Metropolitan Hospital. Participants discussed potential projects, identified challenges, and brainstormed solutions to integrate digital tools with lean practices in their own departments.

Conclusion: Inspiring Change and Innovation

As the session concluded, Dr. Garcia and Dr. Chen commended the team for their enthusiasm and willingness to learn from these inspiring case studies. "By embracing digital tools and integrating them with lean practices, we can drive meaningful change and innovation in healthcare delivery," Dr. Garcia said.

Dr. Chen nodded in agreement, "Let's continue to explore, innovate, and apply these best practices to enhance our operations and deliver exceptional value to our patients. Together, we can lead the way in digital lean transformation."

The healthcare professionals, IT experts, and lean practitioners left the conference room feeling inspired and motivated, ready to harness the power of digital tools and lean principles to drive excellence in healthcare delivery. With a shared vision for the future, Metropolitan Hospital was poised to achieve remarkable success in integrating technology and lean practices.

Challenges of Digital Transformation in Lean

In the high-tech strategy meeting room of Metropolitan Hospital, a group of department heads, lean practitioners, and IT specialists assembled to discuss the challenges they were facing in their journey of digital transformation. Dr. Sofia Garcia and Dr. Michael Chen, as usual, were leading the discussion.

Dr. Garcia began, her tone serious but encouraging, "Good afternoon, everyone. We've made great strides in integrating digital tools with our lean practices, but it's essential to acknowledge and address the challenges we face in this journey. Today, we will discuss these challenges and explore strategies to overcome them."

Dr. Chen added, "Digital transformation is complex, and its intersection with lean practices can present unique obstacles. By identifying these challenges, we can develop solutions that ensure our digital lean initiatives are successful and sustainable."

Challenges of Digital Transformation in Lean:

Dr. Garcia outlined some of the key challenges they were encountering:

1. **Resistance to Change:** "One of the most significant challenges is resistance to change. Our staff is accustomed to traditional workflows, and the shift to digital tools can be daunting. Overcoming this resistance requires effective change management and clear communication about the benefits of digital transformation."
2. **Integration Issues:** "Integrating new digital tools with existing systems can be complex. Incompatible software, data silos, and fragmented processes can hinder the seamless adoption of digital solutions. We need robust IT support and careful planning to ensure smooth integration."
3. **Data Security and Privacy:** "With the increase in digital tools, there's a heightened risk of data breaches and privacy concerns. Ensuring that our systems are secure and compliant with regulations is paramount. We must invest in advanced cybersecurity measures and conduct regular audits."
4. **Cost and Resource Allocation:** "Digital transformation

can be expensive, requiring significant investment in technology, training, and ongoing support. Balancing these costs with our budget constraints is challenging. We must prioritize initiatives that offer the highest return on investment."
5. **Skill Gaps:** "Our staff may lack the necessary skills to effectively use new digital tools. Addressing this skill gap requires comprehensive training programs and ongoing support to ensure everyone is comfortable and proficient with the technology."
6. **Maintaining Lean Principles:** "While focusing on digital transformation, it's crucial not to lose sight of our core lean principles. Ensuring that digital tools enhance rather than hinder our lean practices is a delicate balance."

Interactive Discussion: Overcoming Challenges

Dr. Garcia and Dr. Chen facilitated an open discussion, encouraging participants to share their experiences and ideas for overcoming these challenges. The room buzzed with conversation as department heads, lean practitioners, and IT specialists exchanged insights and brainstormed solutions.

Strategy Session: Developing Solutions

The team broke into smaller groups to develop actionable strategies for addressing each challenge. After an hour of intensive brainstorming, the groups reconvened to share their ideas.

Group 1: Overcoming Resistance to Change

"We propose a comprehensive change management plan that includes regular communication, training, and involvement of key stakeholders in the decision-making process," suggested Sarah, the HR manager. "By highlighting the benefits of digital tools and providing support, we can ease the transition for our staff."

Group 2: Ensuring Seamless Integration

"Our focus will be on selecting compatible systems and developing custom APIs to facilitate integration," said Alex, the IT lead. "We'll also conduct pilot projects to identify and address potential issues before full-scale implementation."

Group 3: Enhancing Data Security and Privacy

"We recommend investing in advanced encryption technologies and implementing strict access controls," said Rachel, the compliance officer. "Regular cybersecurity training for staff and continuous monitoring of our systems will help mitigate risks."

Group 4: Managing Costs and Resources

"We need to prioritize digital initiatives based on their potential impact and ROI," suggested Mark, the CFO. "By starting with pilot projects and scaling successful ones, we can manage costs more effectively."

Group 5: Bridging Skill Gaps

"Comprehensive training programs and ongoing support are essential," said Lisa, the training coordinator. "We propose creating digital learning modules and appointing digital champions within each department to provide on-the-ground assistance."

Group 6: Maintaining Lean Principles

"We must ensure that all digital tools are aligned with our lean principles," emphasized Tom, the lean coordinator. "Regular reviews and feedback loops will help us ensure that digital initiatives support and enhance our lean practices."

Conclusion: A Unified Approach

Dr. Garcia and Dr. Chen were impressed with the team's proactive approach and innovative solutions. "By working together and addressing these challenges head-on, we can ensure the success of our digital transformation journey," Dr. Garcia said.

Dr. Chen added, "Let's implement these strategies and continue to support each other as we navigate this complex but rewarding journey. Together, we can achieve excellence in healthcare delivery through digital lean transformation."

The meeting concluded with a renewed sense of purpose and determination. The team left the strategy meeting room ready to tackle the challenges of digital transformation, confident in their ability to overcome obstacles and drive continuous improvement in healthcare delivery.

Future of Lean in a Digital World

In the grand auditorium of Metropolitan Hospital, the annual Visionary Summit was in full swing. The audience consisted of healthcare professionals, industry leaders, technology innovators, and lean experts. The summit's highlight was the keynote session, "The Future of Lean in a Digital World," led by Dr. Sofia Garcia and Dr. Michael Chen.

Dr. Garcia began, her voice filled with anticipation and vision, "Welcome to the Visionary Summit. Today, we explore the future of lean principles in an increasingly digital world. The integration of technology with lean practices presents unprecedented opportunities and transformative potential."

Dr. Chen continued, "Our goal is to envision how digital advancements will shape the future of lean and to identify strategies for leveraging these technologies to drive operational excellence and superior patient care."

Envisioning the Future: Key Themes

Dr. Garcia and Dr. Chen outlined key themes that would shape the future of lean in a digital world:

1. **AI and Machine Learning:** "Artificial intelligence (AI) and machine learning are revolutionizing data analysis and decision-making," Dr. Garcia explained. "Predictive analytics can anticipate patient needs, optimize resource allocation, and identify areas for improvement, enhancing our lean practices."
2. **Internet of Things (IoT):** "IoT devices provide real-time data on equipment, patient conditions, and environmental factors," Dr. Chen said. "This continuous stream of data enables proactive maintenance, immediate response to patient needs, and more efficient operations."
3. **Robotic Process Automation (RPA):** "RPA can automate repetitive tasks, freeing up staff to focus on value-added activities," Dr. Garcia noted. "By reducing human error and increasing efficiency, RPA supports our lean objectives."
4. **Telehealth and Virtual Care:** "Telehealth expands access to care and reduces the need for physical visits," Dr. Chen highlighted. "Virtual care models enhance patient engagement and allow us to deliver lean, patient-centered care remotely."
5. **Blockchain Technology:** "Blockchain offers secure, transparent, and immutable data management," Dr. Garcia explained. "It can streamline supply chain processes, ensure data integrity, and enhance trust in our systems."
6. **Augmented Reality (AR) and Virtual Reality (VR):**

"AR and VR provide immersive training environments and enhance patient treatment plans," Dr. Chen said. "These technologies can improve skills acquisition and patient outcomes, aligning with our lean goals."

Interactive Visioning: Imagining the Future

The session transitioned into an interactive visioning exercise. Attendees were divided into small groups, each tasked with imagining and designing future scenarios where digital technologies seamlessly integrated with lean principles to create breakthrough improvements in healthcare.

Group 1: AI-Driven Patient Care

"We envision a future where AI-driven systems predict patient needs and personalize treatment plans," Sarah, a senior nurse, shared. "AI can analyze vast amounts of patient data to identify patterns and suggest proactive interventions, improving patient outcomes and reducing waste."

Group 2: IoT-Enabled Smart Hospitals

"Our vision is of a smart hospital where IoT devices continuously monitor equipment health, patient vitals, and environmental conditions," Alex, an IT specialist, explained. "Real-time data can trigger automated responses, such as adjusting room temperatures for patient comfort or alerting staff to maintenance needs, enhancing efficiency and patient care."

Group 3: Robotic Process Automation in Administration

"We see RPA handling administrative tasks like scheduling, billing, and documentation," Rachel, an administrator, suggested. "This automation allows healthcare professionals to focus on patient care and strategic initiatives, aligning with lean's focus on value creation."

Group 4: Expanding Telehealth Services

"We envision expanding telehealth to provide comprehensive remote care, including virtual consultations, remote monitoring, and digital follow-ups," Mark, a physician, proposed. "This approach reduces hospital visits, lowers costs, and improves accessibility, embodying lean's principles of efficiency and patient-centric care."

Group 5: Blockchain in Supply Chain Management

"We imagine a secure, transparent supply chain powered by blockchain technology," Lisa, a supply chain manager, shared. "Blockchain can track every step of the supply chain, ensuring data integrity, reducing fraud, and optimizing inventory management."

Group 6: AR and VR for Training and Treatment

"Our vision includes using AR and VR for immersive training and treatment plans," Tom, a medical trainer, highlighted. "These technologies can provide realistic training environments and enhance patient rehabilitation programs, supporting continuous improvement and skill development."

Conclusion: A Unified Vision for the Future

Dr. Garcia and Dr. Chen listened attentively to each group's presentation, impressed by the innovative ideas and forward-thinking solutions.

"Thank you for your visionary contributions," Dr. Garcia said, addressing the audience. "By embracing these digital advancements and integrating them with our lean principles, we can create a future where healthcare is more efficient, effective, and patient-centered."

Dr. Chen added, "Let's commit to continuous learning and innovation as we navigate this digital transformation journey. Together, we can lead the way in creating a lean, digital future that sets new standards for healthcare excellence."

The Visionary Summit concluded with a sense of excitement and determination. The participants left the auditorium inspired by the possibilities and ready to pioneer the future of lean in a digital world, confident in their ability to drive transformative change in healthcare.

Tools for Digital Lean Implementation

In the bright and modern Innovation Lab of Metropolitan Hospital, Dr. Sofia Garcia and Dr. Michael Chen gathered with a select group of lean practitioners, IT experts, and department leaders. The room was filled with excitement as they prepared to explore the tools essential for digital lean implementation.

Dr. Garcia opened the session with a confident tone, "Welcome, everyone. Today, we will delve into the tools that can help us integrate digital technology with our lean practices. These tools are pivotal for driving efficiency, enhancing patient care, and achieving operational excellence."

Dr. Chen added, "Our objective is to understand how these tools can be effectively implemented and how they align with our lean principles. Let's explore each tool in detail and discuss their potential applications in our hospital."

Exploring Key Tools for Digital Lean Implementation:

1. **Digital Value Stream Mapping (VSM) Tools:**

Dr. Garcia began, "Value stream mapping is fundamental to lean, and digital VSM tools offer enhanced capabilities. Tools like Lucidchart, Miro, and iGrafx enable us to create dynamic, interactive value stream maps. These tools allow real-time collaboration, making it easier to identify bottlenecks and opportunities for improvement."

The group watched a demonstration of Lucidchart, showing how a digital value stream map could be created and shared across departments.

1. **Enterprise Resource Planning (ERP) Systems:**

Dr. Chen highlighted, "ERP systems like SAP, Oracle, and Microsoft Dynamics integrate various business processes, providing a unified view of operations. These systems facilitate better resource planning, inventory management, and data analysis, which are crucial for lean implementation."

An IT expert showcased SAP's capabilities, emphasizing how it could streamline processes and reduce waste in supply chain management.

1. **Customer Relationship Management (CRM) Systems:**

"CRM systems such as Salesforce, HubSpot, and Zoho help manage patient relationships and improve service delivery," Dr. Garcia explained. "These tools enable us to track patient interactions, personalize care, and enhance patient satisfaction, aligning with our lean focus on value creation."

The team viewed a live demo of Salesforce, illustrating how patient data could be managed efficiently to improve engagement and care coordination.

1. **Robotic Process Automation (RPA):**

Dr. Chen continued, "RPA tools like UiPath, Automation Anywhere, and Blue Prism automate repetitive tasks, increasing efficiency and reducing errors. By deploying RPA, we can free up our staff to focus on more value-added activities."

An RPA specialist demonstrated how UiPath could automate administrative tasks such as appointment scheduling and billing, significantly reducing manual workload.

1. **IoT Devices and Analytics Platforms:**

"IoT devices collect real-time data from various sources, and analytics platforms like AWS IoT, Microsoft Azure, and Google Cloud can analyze this data to provide actionable insights," Dr. Garcia noted. "These tools help monitor equipment, track patient vitals, and optimize operations."

The group observed a presentation on Microsoft Azure's IoT suite, showing how real-time data from hospital equipment could be analyzed to predict maintenance needs and prevent downtime.

1. **AI and Machine Learning Tools:**

Dr. Chen emphasized, "AI and machine learning tools such as IBM Watson, TensorFlow, and H2O.ai offer advanced data analysis capabilities. These tools can predict trends, identify inefficiencies, and support decision-making, driving continuous improvement."

The team watched a demonstration of IBM Watson, illustrating how it could analyze patient data to predict outcomes and suggest treatment plans, improving patient care and operational efficiency.

Interactive Workshop: Hands-On with Tools

After the presentations, the session transitioned into an interactive workshop. Participants were divided into small groups, each focusing on a specific tool. They had the opportunity to explore the tool hands-on, guided by experts.

Group 1: Digital VSM Tools

Sarah, a senior nurse, and her group worked with Lucidchart, creating a value stream map for the patient admission process. They identified bottlenecks and brainstormed solutions to streamline the workflow.

Group 2: ERP Systems

Alex, an IT specialist, led his group in exploring SAP. They simulated managing inventory and resource allocation, highlighting how the system could improve efficiency and reduce waste.

Group 3: CRM Systems

Rachel, an administrator, and her group delved into Salesforce, tracking patient interactions and developing strategies to enhance patient engagement and satisfaction.

Group 4: RPA Tools

Mark, a physician, and his group used UiPath to automate appointment scheduling. They were impressed by how much time could be saved, allowing staff to focus on patient care.

Group 5: IoT Devices and Analytics Platforms

Lisa, a supply chain manager, led her group in exploring Microsoft Azure's IoT suite, analyzing data from hospital equipment to predict maintenance needs and optimize operations.

Group 6: AI and Machine Learning Tools

Tom, a medical trainer, and his group experimented with IBM Watson, analyzing patient data to predict outcomes and suggest treatment plans, showcasing the potential for improving patient care.

Conclusion: Embracing Digital Tools for Lean Implementation

Dr. Garcia and Dr. Chen reconvened the group for a final discussion. The participants shared their insights and experiences from the hands-on workshop, expressing enthusiasm for the potential of these tools.

"By leveraging these digital tools, we can enhance our lean practices and drive significant improvements in efficiency and patient care," Dr. Garcia concluded. "Let's commit to integrating these technologies into our operations and continuously seeking ways to innovate."

Dr. Chen added, "The future of lean in a digital world is bright, and with these tools, we can achieve new heights of operational excellence. Together, we will lead the way in transforming healthcare through digital lean implementation."

The session ended with a sense of excitement and determination. The participants left the Innovation Lab equipped with new knowledge and ready to embrace the tools that would drive their digital lean journey, confident in their ability to achieve excellence in healthcare.

15

Chapter 15: Sustaining Lean Improvements

Building a Roadmap for Sustained Lean Success

In the sleek, modern boardroom of Metropolitan Hospital, the leadership team gathered for a crucial strategic planning session. The agenda: building a roadmap for sustained lean success. Dr. Sofia Garcia and Dr. Michael Chen, the hospital's leading lean advocates, stood at the head of the table, ready to guide the team through this critical process.

Dr. Garcia began, her voice steady and confident, "Welcome, everyone. Today, we focus on creating a comprehensive roadmap that ensures our lean improvements are not just implemented but sustained over the long term. Sustaining lean success requires a clear vision, strategic planning, and continuous commitment."

Dr. Chen added, "Our objective is to outline the steps necessary to embed lean principles deeply into our organization's culture and operations. Let's start by identifying the key components of our roadmap."

Key Components of the Roadmap:

1. **Vision and Goals:**

"First, we need a clear vision and specific goals," Dr. Garcia explained. "Our vision should articulate where we want to be in the future and how lean principles will help us get there. Goals must be measurable, achievable, and aligned with our overall mission."

The team brainstormed and drafted a vision statement: "To become a benchmark for excellence in healthcare by integrating lean principles into every aspect of our operations, continuously improving patient care and operational efficiency."

1. **Leadership Commitment:**

"Leadership commitment is crucial," Dr. Chen emphasized. "Our leaders must model lean behaviors, provide ongoing support, and allocate necessary resources. This commitment must be visible and unwavering."

The CEO, Sarah Thompson, pledged her support, "I am fully committed to this initiative. We will ensure that our leadership team receives continuous lean training and that lean principles are embedded in our strategic decision-making processes."

1. **Employee Engagement and Training:**

"Engaging and training our employees is vital," Dr. Garcia noted. "Every staff member must understand the value of lean and their role in sustaining improvements. We will implement comprehensive training programs and encourage active participation."

The HR Director, James Lee, outlined a plan, "We'll develop a training curriculum covering lean fundamentals and advanced topics. We'll also create a recognition program to celebrate lean successes and encourage continuous improvement."

1. **Continuous Improvement Culture:**

"We need to foster a culture of continuous improvement," Dr. Chen said. "This involves encouraging employees to identify improvement opportunities and empowering them to take action. We'll establish a system for capturing and implementing these ideas."

The Quality Improvement Manager, Linda Martinez, proposed, "We'll set up regular Kaizen events and create an online platform for employees to submit improvement ideas. This will ensure a steady flow of innovative solutions."

1. **Performance Metrics and Monitoring:**

"Monitoring our progress with relevant metrics is essential," Dr. Garcia highlighted. "We'll establish key performance indicators (KPIs) to track our lean initiatives and ensure alignment with our goals."

The Operations Manager, Mark Robinson, shared his plan, "We'll use KPIs like cycle time, patient satisfaction, and operational efficiency. Regular reviews will help us stay on track and make necessary adjustments."

1. **Sustainability and Adaptation:**

"Finally, we must focus on sustainability and adaptation," Dr. Chen concluded. "Lean is not a one-time project but an ongoing journey. We must be prepared to adapt our strategies as we grow and evolve."

The IT Director, Jessy Wong, suggested, "We'll leverage digital tools to support our lean initiatives and ensure they remain effective over time. Regular audits and feedback loops will help us adapt and sustain our improvements."

Interactive Planning Workshop: Crafting the Roadmap

The session transitioned into an interactive workshop. Participants were divided into small groups, each tasked with developing detailed action plans for one of the roadmap components.

Group 1: Vision and Goals

Sarah and her team refined the vision statement and set specific, measurable goals for the next five years. They outlined milestones and key deliverables to track progress.

Group 2: Leadership Commitment

James led his group in developing a leadership training program and a communication plan to ensure transparency and consistent messaging across the organization.

Group 3: Employee Engagement and Training

Linda's team created a comprehensive training curriculum and designed a recognition program to celebrate lean achievements and motivate staff.

Group 4: Continuous Improvement Culture

Mark's group proposed a schedule for regular Kaizen events and developed an online platform for idea submission, ensuring continuous employee involvement.

Group 5: Performance Metrics and Monitoring

Jessy's team identified key KPIs and established a regular review process to monitor progress and make data-driven adjustments.

Group 6: Sustainability and Adaptation

Jessy Wong's group planned for the integration of digital tools and developed a framework for regular audits and feedback loops to sustain and adapt lean practices.

Conclusion: Unveiling the Roadmap

Dr. Garcia and Dr. Chen reconvened the group to share their detailed action plans. The room buzzed with energy and optimism as each group presented their strategies.

"Thank you for your dedication and hard work," Dr. Garcia said, addressing the team. "Together, we have built a comprehensive roadmap that will guide us toward sustained lean success. This roadmap is not just a plan but a commitment to continuous improvement and excellence."

Dr. Chen added, "By following this roadmap, we will embed lean principles into our culture and operations, ensuring long-term success and superior patient care. Let's move forward with determination and confidence, knowing that we have the vision and the plan to achieve our goals."

The strategic planning session concluded with a sense of unity and purpose. The leadership team left the boardroom ready to implement the roadmap, confident in their ability to sustain lean improvements and drive Metropolitan Hospital toward a future of operational excellence and outstanding patient care.

Training and Development for Lean

The training room at Metropolitan Hospital buzzed with anticipation. Employees from various departments had gathered for the first session of a comprehensive lean training program. Dr. Sofia Garcia and Dr. Michael Chen stood at the front, ready to lead the initiative.

Dr. Garcia welcomed the participants with a warm smile, "Thank you all for being here. Today marks the beginning of our journey towards embedding lean principles deeply into our daily operations. Training and development are crucial for sustaining our lean improvements, and your involvement is key to our success."

Dr. Chen added, "Our goal is to equip you with the knowledge and skills to implement lean effectively. We want to create a culture where continuous improvement is part of everyone's job."

The Training Curriculum:

1. **Lean Fundamentals:**

Dr. Garcia kicked off the session with a comprehensive overview of lean fundamentals. She explained the core principles, emphasizing the importance of value creation and waste elimination.

"Lean is about delivering maximum value to our patients while minimizing waste," Dr. Garcia stated. "Understanding these fundamentals will help us see our processes through a lean lens."

Participants engaged in interactive discussions, sharing their experiences and identifying areas where they could apply lean principles.

1. **Value Stream Mapping (VSM):**

Dr. Chen led the next segment, focusing on value stream mapping. He introduced digital VSM tools and demonstrated how to create and analyze value stream maps.

"VSM is a powerful tool for visualizing our processes and identifying inefficiencies," Dr. Chen explained. "By mapping our value streams, we can pinpoint areas for improvement and develop targeted solutions."

The attendees worked in groups, using digital tools to map out their respective departments' processes, identifying bottlenecks and brainstorming improvement strategies.

1. **Kaizen and Continuous Improvement:**

Linda Martinez, the Quality Improvement Manager, took the stage to discuss Kaizen and continuous improvement. She shared real-life examples of successful Kaizen events and how they had transformed hospital operations.

"Kaizen is about making small, incremental improvements," Linda said. "It's a philosophy that encourages everyone to look for ways to improve their work. Our goal is to foster a culture where continuous improvement is the norm."

Participants were divided into small groups to simulate a Kaizen event, identifying problems and proposing solutions for a common hospital scenario.

1. **Lean Tools:**

James Lee, the HR Director, introduced various lean tools such as 5S, Kanban, and Poka-Yoke. He explained how these tools could be used to organize workspaces, manage inventory, and prevent errors.

"These tools are essential for creating a lean environment," James noted. "By applying 5S, we can create a more organized and efficient workspace. Kanban helps us manage our workflows, and Poka-Yoke prevents errors, ensuring higher quality."

Participants practiced using these tools in hands-on activities, gaining practical experience that they could apply in their departments.

1. **Leadership and Engagement:**

Sarah Thompson, the CEO, addressed the importance of leadership and employee engagement in sustaining lean improvements. She shared her vision for a lean culture and how leaders at all levels could support this transformation.

"Leadership is about setting the example and providing the support needed for lean initiatives to thrive," Sarah emphasized. "Engaging our employees and involving them in the process is crucial. They are the ones who can identify improvement opportunities and drive change."

The participants discussed strategies for fostering engagement and creating a supportive environment for lean practices.

1. **Performance Metrics and Monitoring:**

Mark Robinson, the Operations Manager, concluded the

CHAPTER 15: SUSTAINING LEAN IMPROVEMENTS

session with a discussion on performance metrics and monitoring. He explained how to set relevant KPIs and use data to drive continuous improvement.

"Metrics are our compass," Mark stated. "They help us understand where we are and where we need to go. By regularly monitoring our performance, we can make informed decisions and ensure we stay on track."

Participants learned how to develop and use dashboards to visualize their performance metrics, making it easier to track progress and identify areas for improvement.

Interactive Workshop: Applying Lean Concepts

The session transitioned into an interactive workshop. Participants worked in small groups, applying the lean concepts they had learned to real-world scenarios within the hospital.

Group 1: Lean Fundamentals

Sarah and her group reviewed the lean principles and discussed how to integrate them into their daily routines. They developed a plan to raise awareness about lean among their colleagues.

Group 2: Value Stream Mapping

Dr. Chen's group created a detailed value stream map of the patient discharge process. They identified several inefficiencies and proposed actionable solutions to streamline the process.

Group 3: Kaizen and Continuous Improvement

Linda's team simulated a Kaizen event focused on reducing patient wait times. They identified root causes and brainstormed improvement ideas, presenting their findings to the larger group.

Group 4: Lean Tools

James' group practiced implementing 5S in a mock storage

area, organizing supplies and creating a more efficient layout. They also experimented with Kanban to manage inventory levels.

Group 5: Leadership and Engagement

Sarah Thompson led her group in developing strategies to engage employees in lean initiatives. They created a communication plan to promote lean principles and encourage participation.

Group 6: Performance Metrics and Monitoring

Mark's group identified key performance metrics for the emergency department. They designed a dashboard to track these metrics and developed a plan for regular performance reviews.

Conclusion: Commitment to Lean Training and Development

Dr. Garcia and Dr. Chen reconvened the group for a final discussion. The participants shared their insights and experiences from the interactive workshop, expressing enthusiasm for applying lean principles in their departments.

"Today's session has been a fantastic start," Dr. Garcia said. "Your engagement and commitment to learning are crucial for our lean journey. Remember, lean is a continuous process. Keep applying what you've learned, and always look for ways to improve."

Dr. Chen added, "Training and development are ongoing. We'll continue to provide opportunities for learning and growth, ensuring that everyone is equipped to contribute to our lean success. Together, we can achieve remarkable improvements."

The training session ended with a sense of unity and determination. The participants left the training center equipped with new knowledge and skills, ready to drive lean initiatives and sustain improvements across Metropolitan Hospital.

Continuous Assessment and Adjustment

In the bright and spacious conference room of Metropolitan Hospital, the leadership team gathered for their quarterly review meeting. This session was dedicated to assessing the progress of their lean initiatives and making necessary adjustments. Dr. Sofia Garcia and Dr. Michael Chen, the driving forces behind the lean transformation, prepared to lead the discussion.

Dr. Garcia opened the meeting, her voice filled with determination, "Good morning, everyone. Today, we will review our lean initiatives, assess their impact, and identify areas where we need to make adjustments. Continuous assessment and adjustment are crucial to sustaining our lean success."

Dr. Chen added, "Our goal is to ensure that we are on the right track and to make data-driven decisions for further improvement. Let's start by reviewing our key performance indicators (KPIs)."

Reviewing Key Performance Indicators (KPIs):

1. **Operational Efficiency:**

Mark Robinson, the Operations Manager, presented the first set of data. "We've seen a significant reduction in cycle times and lead times in several departments," he reported. "However, the emergency department is still facing challenges."

The team analyzed the data, identifying bottlenecks and discussing possible solutions. "We need to dig deeper into the root causes," Dr. Garcia suggested. "Let's organize a Kaizen event specifically for the emergency department."

1. **Patient Satisfaction:**

Linda Martinez, the Quality Improvement Manager, shared the patient satisfaction scores. "Overall, our scores have improved, but there are still concerns about waiting times and communication in certain areas."

The team discussed strategies to enhance patient communication and reduce wait times. "We should implement a real-time feedback system to address issues promptly," Dr. Chen proposed.

1. **Financial Performance:**

James Lee, the HR Director, presented the financial performance metrics. "We've achieved cost savings in several areas, but we need to ensure these savings are sustainable."

The team reviewed the cost-saving initiatives and identified opportunities for further efficiency. "We should focus on reducing waste in our procurement process," Mark suggested. "Let's conduct a value stream mapping session to identify inefficiencies."

Interactive Discussion: Adjusting Lean Initiatives

The meeting transitioned into an interactive discussion. Participants were divided into small groups to brainstorm adjustments to their lean initiatives based on the review.

Group 1: Emergency Department Improvements

Mark led his group in analyzing the data for the emergency department. They identified key issues, including patient flow and staffing levels, and proposed targeted Kaizen events to address these challenges.

Group 2: Enhancing Patient Communication

Linda's group focused on improving patient communication. They developed a plan to implement a real-time feedback system and enhance staff training on patient interaction.

Group 3: Sustainable Cost Savings

James' group reviewed the cost-saving initiatives and identified areas for further improvement. They proposed a value stream mapping session for the procurement process to reduce waste and increase efficiency.

Group 4: Monitoring and Feedback

Jessy Wong, the IT Director, led her group in developing a system for continuous monitoring and feedback. They designed a digital dashboard to track real-time performance metrics and provide instant feedback to staff.

Group 5: Staff Engagement and Training

Sarah Thompson's group focused on staff engagement and training. They proposed additional training sessions and workshops to ensure all employees are equipped with lean skills and knowledge.

Group 6: Leadership and Support

Dr. Garcia and Dr. Chen led their group in discussing how leadership could provide ongoing support for lean initiatives. They developed a plan for regular leadership training and communication to reinforce lean principles.

Conclusion: Commitment to Continuous Improvement

Dr. Garcia and Dr. Chen reconvened the group for a final discussion. The participants shared their insights and proposed adjustments, expressing a strong commitment to continuous improvement.

"Today's review has been incredibly productive," Dr. Garcia said. "Your willingness to analyze data and make necessary adjustments is key to our lean journey. Remember, continuous assessment and adjustment are essential for sustaining our success."

Dr. Chen added, "Lean is a dynamic process. We must remain vigilant, always seeking ways to improve and adapt. By continuously assessing our performance and making data-driven adjustments, we will achieve our goals and maintain our commitment to excellence."

The quarterly review meeting ended with a renewed sense of purpose. The leadership team left the conference room with clear action plans, ready to implement the proposed adjustments and drive continuous improvement across Metropolitan Hospital.

Leadership Commitment to Lean

The early morning sun streamed through the large windows of the conference room at the Mountainview Resort. The tranquil setting provided the perfect backdrop for the hospital leadership team's annual retreat. This year's focus: reinforcing their commitment to Lean principles. Dr. Sofia Garcia and Dr. Michael Chen, the champions of the hospital's Lean transformation, stood at the helm, ready to guide the day's discussions.

Dr. Garcia addressed the group with a confident smile,

"Welcome, everyone. This retreat is about reaffirming our commitment to Lean and ensuring that as leaders, we are fully equipped to drive and sustain this transformation."

Dr. Chen added, "Leadership commitment is the cornerstone of our Lean journey. Without your dedication and active involvement, our efforts cannot succeed. Today, we will explore what it means to be a Lean leader and how we can collectively support our teams."

Exploring Lean Leadership:

1. **Vision and Strategy:**

Sarah Thompson, the CEO, began the session by sharing her vision for the hospital's Lean future. "Our vision is to become a model of operational excellence in healthcare," she declared. "To achieve this, we need a clear strategy that aligns with Lean principles."

The team discussed the strategic goals and how they could be integrated into daily operations. "We need to ensure that every decision we make supports our Lean vision," Mark Robinson, the Operations Manager, emphasized.

1. **Leading by Example:**

James Lee, the HR Director, spoke next about the importance of leading by example. "As leaders, our actions set the tone for the entire organization," he said. "We must embody Lean principles in everything we do."

Dr. Garcia nodded in agreement, "It's not just about what we say but what we do. When our staff sees us practicing Lean, it reinforces their own commitment."

1. **Empowering Employees:**

Linda Martinez, the Quality Improvement Manager, led a discussion on empowering employees. "Lean is about harnessing the collective intelligence of our staff," she explained. "We must create an environment where everyone feels empowered to suggest improvements."

The group brainstormed ways to foster an empowering culture. "Regular feedback sessions and open communication channels are essential," Dr. Chen suggested. "We need to listen to our staff and act on their insights."

1. **Providing Support and Resources:**

Jessy Wong, the IT Director, highlighted the need for providing support and resources. "To sustain Lean, we must invest in the necessary tools and training," she stated. "This includes digital tools for real-time data monitoring and continuous learning opportunities."

The team agreed on the importance of ongoing training and resource allocation. "Our staff needs to feel supported in their Lean efforts," Sarah Thompson added. "We must provide the resources they need to succeed."

Interactive Workshops: Strengthening Leadership Commitment

The retreat transitioned into interactive workshops designed to strengthen leadership commitment to Lean. Participants engaged in hands-on activities and discussions.

Workshop 1: Vision and Strategy Alignment

Sarah Thompson led a workshop on aligning vision and

strategy with Lean principles. Leaders worked in small groups to develop actionable plans for their departments, ensuring that every goal aligned with the hospital's Lean vision.

Workshop 2: Leading by Example

James Lee facilitated a session on leading by example. Leaders shared personal commitments to embodying Lean principles and created accountability partners to support each other in their Lean journeys.

Workshop 3: Empowering Employees

Linda Martinez guided a workshop on empowering employees. Leaders developed strategies for creating an inclusive environment where staff felt encouraged to share ideas and take ownership of Lean initiatives.

Workshop 4: Providing Support and Resources

Jessy Wong led a session on providing support and resources. Leaders identified the tools and training needed for their teams and created plans to ensure these resources were available.

Panel Discussion: Overcoming Challenges in Lean Leadership

The final session of the retreat was a panel discussion featuring leaders who had successfully navigated challenges in their Lean journeys. Dr. Garcia and Dr. Chen moderated the discussion, drawing insights from their experiences.

Mark Robinson: Overcoming Resistance

Mark shared how he overcame resistance to Lean in his department. "It was about building trust and showing the benefits of Lean through small wins," he explained. "Once people saw the positive impact, they were more willing to embrace the changes."

Linda Martinez: Sustaining Momentum

Linda discussed strategies for sustaining momentum. "We celebrate successes, no matter how small," she said. "This keeps the energy high and reminds everyone of the value of our Lean efforts."

Jessy Wong: Leveraging Technology

Jessy highlighted the role of technology in sustaining Lean. "Digital tools have been game-changers," she noted. "They provide real-time data and insights that help us make informed decisions and drive continuous improvement."

Conclusion: Renewed Commitment to Lean Leadership

Dr. Garcia and Dr. Chen reconvened the group for a closing discussion. The participants shared their key takeaways and reaffirmed their commitment to Lean leadership.

"Today has been an inspiring and valuable experience," Dr. Garcia said. "Your dedication and willingness to lead by example are critical to our Lean journey. Let's continue to support each other and our teams, driving sustainable improvements across our organization."

Dr. Chen added, "Leadership commitment is the foundation of Lean success. Together, we can create a culture of continuous improvement and operational excellence. Thank you for your commitment and hard work."

The retreat ended with a renewed sense of purpose and unity. The leadership team left the Mountainview Resort with clear action plans and a strengthened resolve to lead their Lean initiatives, ensuring that Metropolitan Hospital would continue to thrive and excel in its Lean journey.

Recognizing and Rewarding Lean Efforts

The auditorium buzzed with anticipation as staff from all departments gathered for the Annual Excellence Awards Ceremony at Metropolitan Hospital. The event was a highlight of the year, celebrating the hard work and dedication of employees who had excelled in Lean initiatives. The stage was adorned with banners reading "Excellence in Lean," and a table laden with trophies and certificates gleamed under the spotlights.

Dr. Sofia Garcia and Dr. Michael Chen, dressed in their formal attire, stood at the podium, ready to kick off the ceremony. Dr. Garcia began with a warm smile, "Good evening, everyone. Tonight, we gather to recognize and reward the outstanding efforts of our staff in driving Lean improvements. Your hard work and dedication are the heart of our success."

Celebrating Success:

1. **Opening Remarks:**

Dr. Chen continued, "Lean is more than just a set of tools and techniques; it's a culture of continuous improvement and excellence. Each of you has played a crucial role in this journey, and tonight we celebrate your achievements."

The audience applauded, their excitement palpable as they awaited the announcements.

1. **Team Awards:**

The first category of awards was for team achievements. Mark

Robinson, the Operations Manager, stepped up to present the awards. "The first award goes to the Emergency Department team for their exceptional work in reducing patient wait times by 30%," he announced. The team, beaming with pride, made their way to the stage to receive their trophies and certificates.

Next, Linda Martinez, the Quality Improvement Manager, presented the award for the Best Kaizen Event. "This year, the Best Kaizen Event award goes to the Radiology Department for their innovative workflow improvements, which increased efficiency by 25%," she said. The Radiology team accepted their award amid enthusiastic applause.

1. **Individual Awards:**

Dr. Garcia then took the podium to present individual awards. "The first individual award is for Lean Innovator of the Year," she announced. "This award goes to Jessy Wong, our IT Director, for her exceptional work in integrating digital tools with Lean practices, significantly enhancing our data-driven decision-making capabilities."

Jessy Wong walked to the stage, accepting her award with a proud smile. "Thank you," she said. "This recognition means a lot, and it's a testament to the collaborative efforts of our entire team."

Dr. Chen presented the award for Lean Leader of the Year. "This award goes to James Lee, our HR Director, for his outstanding leadership in promoting Lean principles and empowering our staff to drive continuous improvement," he announced.

James Lee accepted his award, acknowledging the support of his colleagues. "Lean is a team effort," he said. "This award is for all of us who believe in the power of continuous improvement."

1. **Special Recognition:**

Sarah Thompson, the CEO, stepped forward to present the final award of the evening. "The Special Recognition Award goes to Dr. Sofia Garcia and Dr. Michael Chen for their relentless dedication and visionary leadership in spearheading our Lean transformation," she announced, to resounding applause.

Dr. Garcia and Dr. Chen accepted the award together. Dr. Garcia spoke on behalf of both, "Thank you. This journey has been incredibly rewarding, and it's all because of the hard work and commitment of every single one of you. Together, we are making a difference."

Interactive Segment: Sharing Success Stories

After the formal awards ceremony, the event transitioned into an interactive segment where award recipients shared their success stories.

Emergency Department Team:

Mark Robinson and his team detailed their efforts to reduce patient wait times. "We focused on streamlining our triage process and improving communication between departments," Mark explained. "By doing so, we were able to significantly cut down on waiting periods."

Radiology Department:

The Radiology team shared their journey of workflow improvements. "We held several Kaizen events to identify bottlenecks and implement changes," one team member recounted. "The result was a 25% increase in efficiency, which had a huge impact on our service delivery."

Jessy Wong discussed the integration of digital tools with Lean practices. "Implementing real-time data dashboards has transformed our decision-making process," she said. "We can now quickly identify issues and respond proactively, ensuring continuous improvement."

James Lee spoke about his approach to Lean leadership. "Empowering our staff has been key," he emphasized. "When employees feel valued and involved, they're more motivated to contribute to our Lean initiatives."

Conclusion: A Night to Remember

As the evening drew to a close, Dr. Garcia and Dr. Chen returned to the stage for the final remarks. "Tonight has been a celebration of your hard work and dedication," Dr. Garcia said. "Recognizing and rewarding Lean efforts is essential to sustaining our momentum and fostering a culture of continuous improvement."

Dr. Chen added, "Your achievements inspire us all. Let's carry this spirit forward, continuing to strive for excellence in everything we do. Thank you for your unwavering commitment to Lean."

The Annual Excellence Awards Ceremony ended with a standing ovation, the room filled with a sense of pride and accomplishment. The staff left the auditorium, energized and motivated to continue their Lean journey, knowing that their efforts were recognized and appreciated.

Case Studies: Long-Term Lean Success Stories

In the hushed atmosphere of the Metropolitan Hospital boardroom, the hospital's leadership team gathered for their quarterly strategy review meeting. As they settled into their seats, the anticipation was palpable. Dr. Sofia Garcia and Dr. Michael Chen, the champions of the hospital's Lean transformation, stood at the head of the table, ready to share long-term Lean success stories.

Dr. Garcia began, her voice filled with pride, "Good morning, everyone. Today, we'll be discussing some of our long-term Lean success stories—initiatives that have not only achieved significant improvements but have also sustained their impact over time."

Dr. Chen added, "These case studies serve as powerful examples of what can be accomplished with dedication, perseverance, and a commitment to Lean principles. Let's dive in and explore the journeys of these remarkable initiatives."

Case Study 1: Emergency Department Optimization

Mark Robinson, the Operations Manager, led the discussion on the Emergency Department Optimization initiative. "Several years ago, our emergency department was facing severe overcrowding and long wait times," he began. "We embarked on a Lean journey to streamline processes and improve patient flow."

Mark shared the key strategies implemented, including:

- **Value Stream Mapping:** Identifying bottlenecks and waste in the patient journey.
- **Kaizen Events:** Implementing rapid improvement projects to address specific issues.

- **Staff Training:** Equipping employees with Lean tools and methodologies.
- **Continuous Monitoring:** Regularly tracking performance metrics to sustain improvements.

"The results have been remarkable," Mark continued. "We've seen a 40% reduction in patient wait times and a significant increase in patient satisfaction scores. These improvements have been sustained over the long term, demonstrating the lasting impact of our Lean efforts."

Case Study 2: Lean Supply Chain Management

James Lee, the HR Director, presented the case study on Lean Supply Chain Management. "Our supply chain was once plagued by inefficiencies, leading to delays and increased costs," he explained. "Through a comprehensive Lean initiative, we transformed our supply chain processes to drive efficiency and responsiveness."

James outlined the key components of the initiative:

- **Just-in-Time (JIT) Inventory:** Minimizing inventory levels to reduce waste and improve agility.
- **Kanban System:** Implementing visual signaling to streamline inventory replenishment.
- **Supplier Collaboration:** Building strong partnerships with suppliers to enhance reliability and responsiveness.
- **Continuous Improvement:** Engaging employees in ongoing problem-solving and process refinement.

"The results speak for themselves," James declared. "We've achieved a 30% reduction in procurement costs and a 50% decrease in lead times. These improvements have not only optimized our operations but have also strengthened our relationships with suppliers, driving long-term sustainability."

Case Study 3: Lean Culture Transformation

Linda Martinez, the Quality Improvement Manager, shared insights into the hospital's Lean Culture Transformation initiative. "Creating a Lean culture is about more than just implementing tools; it's about fostering a mindset of continuous improvement and empowerment," she emphasized.

Linda highlighted the key elements of the initiative:

- **Leadership Commitment:** Demonstrating visible support and engagement from hospital leadership.
- **Employee Engagement:** Empowering staff to participate in problem-solving and decision-making.
- **Training and Development:** Providing ongoing education and development opportunities in Lean principles.
- **Recognition and Rewards:** Celebrating successes and acknowledging contributions to Lean initiatives.

"Our journey to build a Lean culture has been transformative," Linda stated. "Employees at all levels are actively engaged in driving improvements, and Lean principles have become ingrained in our organizational DNA. This cultural shift has not only led to tangible operational improvements but has also enhanced employee morale and satisfaction, laying the foundation for sustained success."

Conclusion: Lessons Learned and Future Outlook

As the discussion drew to a close, Dr. Garcia and Dr. Chen reflected on the valuable lessons learned from these long-term Lean success stories. "These case studies exemplify the power of Lean principles to drive sustained improvement and excellence," Dr. Garcia remarked. "By embracing Lean as a way of life and continuously striving for better, we can achieve lasting success in our pursuit of operational excellence."

Dr. Chen added, "As we look to the future, let these success stories inspire us to continue our Lean journey with renewed vigor and determination. Together, we will build upon our achievements and create a legacy of excellence for generations to come."

The leadership team left the boardroom, energized and inspired by the enduring impact of Lean on Metropolitan Hospital's operations. Armed with valuable insights from these long-term success stories, they were ready to chart the course for continued improvement and innovation in the years ahead.

About the Author

Goodson Mumba is a multifaceted individual known for his diverse expertise and prolific contributions across various fields. As an infopreneur, thought leader, and spiritual leader, he has inspired countless individuals through his insightful teachings and impactful writings. Mumba is also an accomplished author, with several notable works to his name, including "Understanding Corporate Worship," "The Years I Spent in a Week," "Management By Harmony," "The CEO's Diary," "Change to Change" and "Creative Thinking for results" His literary works span topics ranging from business management to personal development and spirituality, reflecting his broad range of interests and insights.

With a Master of Business Leadership (MBL) and a Bachelor of Arts in Theology (BTh), Mumba brings a unique blend of business acumen and spiritual wisdom to his work. His educational background is further enriched by a Group Diploma in Management Studies, providing him with a solid foundation in organizational dynamics and leadership principles. Additionally, Mumba holds diplomas in Education Psychology, Leadership and Management Styles, Organizational Behaviour, Financial Accounting, Economic Growth and Development, and Project Management, showcasing his commitment to continuous learning and professional development.

Mumba's expertise extends beyond traditional academic disciplines, encompassing areas such as Neuro-Linguistic Programming (NLP) and Positive Psychology. His diverse skill set is complemented by a range of certifications, including Creative Problem Solving and Decision Making, Life Coaching Fundamentals and Techniques, Professional Life Coaching, and Performance Management System Design. These certifications reflect Mumba's dedication to equipping himself with the tools and knowledge necessary to empower others and drive positive change.

As an author, Mumba's writings reflect his deep understanding of human nature, organizational dynamics, and spiritual principles. His works offer practical insights, actionable strategies, and inspirational guidance for individuals seeking personal growth, professional success, and spiritual fulfillment. Mumba's holistic approach to life and leadership resonates with readers worldwide, making him a respected figure in both the business and spiritual communities.

Overall, Goodson Mumba's diverse background, extensive knowledge, and profound insights make him a sought-after speaker, mentor, and author. His commitment to excellence, lifelong learning, and service to others continues to inspire individuals to unlock their full potential and lead lives of purpose and significance.

Goodson Mumba is renowned for initiating the concept of Management by Harmony, revolutionizing traditional management practices with a focus on balanced and holistic approaches. He has authored two influential books on this subject: "Introduction to Management by Harmony" and its sequel, "Management by Harmony."

Mumba's work has significantly impacted the field, offering innovative strategies for fostering organizational harmony and efficiency. His contributions continue to shape contemporary management theories and practices.

www.ingramcontent.com/pod-product-compliance
Lightning Source LLC
Chambersburg PA
CBHW071826210526
45479CB00001B/7